The Numinous Factor

Also by John Walker

Finding God in the Quantum

The Mind of the Mystic

The Numinous Factor

The Spiritual Basis of Science and of Life

John L. Walker, PhD

BALBOA.
PRESS
A DIVISION OF HAY HOUSE

ISBN: 978-1-4525-5767-0 (sc)
ISBN: 978-1-4525-5768-7 (e)
ISBN: 978-1-4525-5769-4 (hc)

Library of Congress Control Number: 2012915582

Balboa Press books may be ordered through booksellers or by contacting:

Balboa Press
A Division of Hay House
1663 Liberty Drive
Bloomington, IN 47403
www.balboapress.com
1-(877) 407-4847

Because of the dynamic nature of the Internet, any web addresses or links contained in this book may have changed since publication and may no longer be valid. The views expressed in this work are solely those of the author and do not necessarily reflect the views of the publisher, and the publisher hereby disclaims any responsibility for them.

The author of this book does not dispense medical advice or prescribe the use of any technique as a form of treatment for physical, emotional, or medical problems without the advice of a physician, either directly or indirectly. The intent of the author is only to offer information of a general nature to help you in your quest for emotional and spiritual well-being. In the event you use any of the information in this book for yourself, which is your constitutional right, the author and the publisher assume no responsibility for your actions.

Any people depicted in stock imagery provided by Thinkstock are models, and such images are being used for illustrative purposes only.
Certain stock imagery © Thinkstock.

Printed in the United States of America

Balboa Press rev. date: 09/11/2012

To Corky
and to Geoff

Table of Contents

Preface

This is a spiritual book. It suggests ways by which all of us can expand our spiritual consciousness to unlimited awareness of the true nature of everything in this complex Universe, from the subatomic world to beyond the outer reaches of space, as well as find more fulfillment in our daily lives. It proposes certain principles that we can factor into our own awareness and thought processes to whatever extent we choose in order to achieve as high a level of spirituality as we are ready to attain. And it shows how using these principles, referred to collectively as The Numinous Factor, can dispel the personal fears and uncertainties about life and death that mankind has taken for granted up to now.

However, we have to clarify at the outset what this book is not. It is not a religious book. There will be no discussions of belief groups, with their different dogmas, creeds, standards, methods of worship, clothing, foods, and names for Deity, since one function of religion is to separate and compartmentalize rather than to unite everyone into one big whole as spirituality tends to do.

Also, this is not a scientific book. Generally-accepted scientific observations will be used as launching pads for discussions of their spiritual natures and components, but nothing will be proven or advocated logically. There is no math and there are no formulas except the famous one from Albert Einstein that everyone already knows. There is, therefore, no required knowledge of science. Everyone is on the same footing here.

Likewise, it is not a scholarly book filled with logical conclusions synthesized from extensive research. Indeed, it prefers to show how our limited human knowledge and narrow reasoning ability cannot fathom the reality of what is out there, or even grasp what most of the Universe is like without recognizing its essentially spiritual nature.

And, finally, it is not a philosophical book, with detailed discussions of various "-isms." Of course, those familiar with such concepts as transcendence versus immanence, theism versus pantheism, monism versus dualism, and especially with the newer term panentheism, will see these in the discussion, but not in abstract. Instead, we will be taking a new tack, a practical one, incorporating (as would be expected) all such aspects of thought, experience, and spirituality into one. Again, the functions of both religion and philosophy are to separate and compartmentalize, much as how a prism breaks down light into a rainbow of colors. The display of individual hues is beautiful, pleasing, and interesting, but the greatest light comes when they are again fused into pure white. Fusing the material world together with the spiritual one within ourselves requires an effort beyond human separatist rationality.

So a mode of understanding beyond human senses and thinking abilities will be introduced and everything will be seen through this mode. Human thinking ability and human knowledge, great as they are, establish such limits to total understanding that we simply must get around these for proper expansion of consciousness. There comes a time when scholarship needs to rise to the point of recognizing its own inadequacy, and achieving this point is one of the first steps in escaping from our human limitations of thought and understanding.

This book, then, is not meant to prove anything, but rather to indicate a spiritual path that is worth a try, a path that could lead to a heightened ability to receive inspiration. Grasping and using the Numinous Factor is one way to rise to new realizations. This book shows methods and insights that we can use to see and appreciate the Spirituality that is actually the basis of all that exists. Using its guidance, we can embark on a voyage to higher consciousness, to greater understanding of ourselves and of everything around us, and to spiritual unity. It can be a glorious journey, leading to complete happiness and peace as we see what the Universe really is and who we ourselves really are.

CHAPTER ONE

- - - - - - - - -

The Need and the Mode

The Problem

With all of the marvelous advances in knowledge of the Universe being made these days, it could be thought that scientists have finally figured out the essential nature of its functions and how it came into being, and that there is, then, no need for consideration of the role of a Divine Creator in all of it. After all, scientists have studied the Big Bang theory, have looked at the expanding universe, have analyzed black holes, have figured out the formation of carbon and other elements needed for life as we know it, and have learned much of how atomic theory works in outer space. They also have come to understand much about the quantum or subatomic world, such as what makes up atoms, what the energy fields are that seem to give rise to everything that exists, and what seems to be the fundamental basis of everything that we can observe and even what we cannot observe. They think that they are getting close to the Theory of Everything that will explain the totality of Creation. It even seems possible that, across the Universe, all energies can balance each other out, leaving no restrictions on the continuity of all of the above phenomena, which might suggest that entities could actually spring into being spontaneously without any need for a spiritual Creator. This seems to solve the whole story of Creativity and to end all the religious speculation.

Yet, there still seem to be a few questions that science has not been able to answer so far:

Where did energy and matter come from in the first place? How and why did this Universe, with its enormous complexity, organization, and delicate balances of enormous forces, get assembled into this form? How did the forces that govern it come into being? What is gravity? What is life? What instigates universes to form? What is outside the Universe? And, more importantly for us personally: Who are we? Why are we here? Where are we going?

We can never get to the bottom of Creation rationally. There is always more to know. The fact is that there are parts of the physical sciences that cannot be seen rationally because that is the way they seem to be set up in relation to us. At the same time, we have yet to understand the Creation through religion since religions throughout human history have come up with a great variety of supposed explanations, usually based on limited knowledge and restricted views of the Supreme Deity.

Viewpoints of the Creation seem to fall into two general categories. In one, the Universe is seen as a strictly physical entity and its origins and operations can be understood rationally without any need for Deity. In the other, the Universe is seen as having been brought into existence by a Creator Who put the breath of life into it, and then either controls it still or has left it to run on its own. Both views, however, indicate that the physical Universe operates as a separate entity, whether created by Deity or not.

Actually, there is another possibility.

Maybe there is a Creative Power that really *is* the energy, *is* the gravity, *is* the rock, *and is* the fusion process in the stars. Maybe there is no separation between the Creator and the Created, between Spiritual and Physical. Maybe everything that we see or measure physically and everything that we might sense or feel spiritually is really One, a Unity. If this is so, then Spirituality, a human term referring to an awareness of the Presence of the Divine, cannot be left out of scientific reasoning. At the same time, science can enhance an understanding of the concrete aspects of the spiritual. The combination of science and spirituality might give a more complete view, similar to how using two eyes gives a perspective that using one eye does not. It would also be reassuring to realize that Deity is not off somewhere doing something else after abandoning us here, but rather exists in, through, and as everything in the Universe, including us, so that there is no separation between man and spirit, a concept that could end the great angst that grips much of the religious world as it tries to find a way to live on after bodily death. It would seem that such a realization could bring us great peace and fulfillment, both in this life and in the next.

This book shows a way to achieve this realization of Divinity as the Essence, the Source, and the Totality of all that is, a viewpoint that leads us to a more complete understanding both of the physical and of the spiritual. The aim here is to present a method that can let us understand better the things around us-our physical world, the vastness of outer space, the tiny world of the atom, the existence of intelligent human beings here and possibly elsewhere, our unexpected and complex added dimensions-by seeing spirituality as the oneness of everything.

Spirituality

Let us see how that can be. We start by remembering that the word "spiritual" (with its roots in "wind" or "breath") refers to the active Divine essence that gives life and animation to physical things. It is generally thought of as being separate from the objects it animates, but for our purposes, we can ponder how spirituality might rather be seen as the totality of the objects. Possibly we can begin to realize that everything is completely spiritual, not just consisting of separate entities that are animated by a special breath. Spiritual and physical, we might decide, along with any other aspects, form a Oneness, a Unity. This book will suggest several steps that the reader might follow to increase awareness of the Presence of Spirituality in everything seen or known, and extending to things not yet seen or known. You may wish to select other such steps, because those listed here constitute just one way of opening the awareness. We will call the steps listed here "The Numinous Factor," since the word "numinous" is not a religious name for Deity, but rather refers to an awareness of the spirituality inherent in everything. We will examine the full meaning of the word "numinous" later on.

Once we have pondered the principles of The Numinous Factor, we will take them first into the subatomic world, where we will see the wild and wonderful ways it carries on its role in life as the basis of everything around us, and then travel out through the cosmos, those vast reaches of outer space, where we will see in more dimensions than we thought we even possessed how all of it developed and why it is the way it is. After that, and actually throughout the discussion, we will develop a different view of the social world in which we now live and of ourselves, seeing a little more of whom we are and what we can become. We might then achieve a greater perspective, a more complete picture of Life Itself, than we have had so far, and thereby achieve peace, fulfillment, and joy as we realize that we are inseparable parts of the Divine Totality.

Awareness of all of this can be achieved through simple explanations along with thoughts for us to ponder, all enhanced by methods that will allow a free flow of intuition that can let enlightenment to blossom within us. There will be no math, no equations, and no complicated concepts. These are means that scientists use to create orderly, balanced, and complete representations of what they are learning. They use scientific methods with what they hope is complete objectivity, employing exact measurements, elimination of variables, logical deduction, and synthesis of accurate conclusions, all of which need to be done in ways that can be duplicated by others. In this book, however, we will be balancing spirituality and science using subjectivity, intuition, insight, and individual conclusions. All these might not be the same for others even if they use our exact methods because spirituality is an individual thing that generally cannot be proven while it is also a unity that sees all things as individual facets of the whole. We will look at why this must be so later on. For now, let us just say that the final awareness will be the same for everyone eventually, but the methods to achieve it will be individualized and subjective.

Actually, this blending of the subjective and objective is what science is all about anyway. For example, as we will see in our look at quantum physics, various observers of quantum phenomena can arrive at different conclusions, all of which are valid, and all of which are part of the system. There is a subjectivity built into our most fundamental area of physics. Even our system of mathematics itself, seemingly solid, dependable, and unchanging, is based on certain axioms that were chosen long ago, and mathematicians have found that alternative systems based on other axioms will work just as well. So everything in science is just a little bit subjective as well as objective in the first place, and our look at it will just try to illuminate it all a little better.

To begin our study of the Numinous, the spirituality in everything, we need to develop an approach that will put us into the proper subjective mode just as the scientific method does for the objective mode. This can be one of the most exciting parts of this journey. Imagine a way of living and seeing life that will raise us above petty earthly viewpoints and squabbles to a higher consciousness wherein all is beauty and peace! And we can start developing it today, right now! To do so, we will enlist a guide whose name forms an acronym that will make the steps of our development easy to remember: EMILY.

EMILY

The letters of EMILY stand for five principles that we can begin to use right now, not only to further our awareness of the Numinous, but to bring greater warmth and comfort to our present lives. The more we practice them, the more we will find ourselves released from the earthly dependencies, uncertainties, and fears that beset us daily. Even when practiced in simple ways, the principles can raise us to a new consciousness that will help us stand firm in spirituality while the rigors of the world buffet us. And the name of our guide, EMILY, will remind us constantly of these principles, which are: Enlightenment, Meditation, Intention, LOVE, and Yielding.

Before we look more closely at these principles, let us see a rationale for using such a guide. We may have seen a demonstration on communication wherein a speaker goes into the audience to show everyone a picture up close. He stands in the middle of the group and holds up a poster with the picture on both sides so all can see it clearly. He then goes back up front and puts up a large version on an easel and asks people to tell what they see. Some of the people start to comment that it is a picture of an ugly witch, where others contend that it is a beautiful girl. The discussion can get quite heated, with people even going up front to point out the features of what they discern, but it is to no avail as the others do not budge from what they think that they discern. Gradually, it dawns on everyone that the people in front are seeing one thing, and the people in the back another, with a distinct dividing line between the two views. What the speaker did, of course, was to show two different pictures, one clearly of a young girl to the front of the audience, the other clearly of a witch to the back half, with the picture he put up front being a clever blending of the two. The point was that people could only see one image in the composite, namely the first one presented to them, despite the arguments given by the other group. We human beings tend to see what we have been programmed to see, so a change of mode will free us to experience higher vibrations and, thus, a heightened sense of the Numinous.

So for the study in this book, we need to let go of the normal human viewpoints that we now accept without question, and adopt different ones to get us into a new realm of visualization. In essence, we need to see all possible views of the composite picture. It is not always easy to make this change. The study of foreign languages, for instance, shows us that there are different ways to express the same thoughts equally well. In English, we may say: "I like it." In Spanish, the wording would be: "It pleases me." Which is correct? Each just has a distinct flavor. The English version puts me as the center of attention in the sentence; the Spanish puts the object in the center. English-speaking students, however, often have a very hard time seeing and using the different meaning and word order of the Spanish sentence even after years of study. In like manner, it might be difficult for some readers of this book to move into the subjective mode of understanding the Universe, but just as we do not have to give up our core language in order to see and maybe even appreciate and learn from another way of expressing something, we do not have to give up our core beliefs to use the Numinous Factor.

Instead, we can follow the steps shown to us by EMILY to see our world and the heavens from a new perspective. Probably each of us will do this in a slightly different way since we are all individuals. But it can be done. We remember that spirituality is a daily decision anyway. No one forces us to be spiritual rather than worldly in our daily outlook. So what we will do here is look at some possibilities, and then our personal decision-making processes can take us to something new. Our viewpoint is our viewpoint and that is how things are. We will just see how to use a new way of looking to develop a different perspective.

Seeds grow best in fertile ground and with proper care. Just as a candle flame cannot exist in an atmosphere devoid of the elements that support it, so a view of spirituality as the basis of the Universe does not exist in an atmosphere devoid of nutrients for it. So we need to establish a mode or a system of preparation before we jump into our study, much like how running a good race depends on steps taken beforehand, such as proper training, the building of endurance, good diet, correct stretching, and good mental conditioning. In the same vein, since schooling and preparation are needed to understand scientific concepts, such as learning the scientific method itself and acquiring basic background information through study and problem solving, there are certain steps that we can take to prepare ourselves for seeing Spirituality as the basis of everything, such as understanding the method itself and acquiring basic background information. The difference is that our spiritual enlightenment will depend on opening ourselves to the information and inspirations already operating in our inner spiritual selves. Our guide, EMILY, will remind us constantly of the five steps or procedures that we can use to uncover this. EMILY, then, will represent: Enlightenment, Meditation, Intention, LOVE, and Yielding. Let us look all of these in a little detail.

Enlightenment

Enlightenment, the first step, establishes our goal and keeps it steadily before us. We can remember the story of the farmer teaching his son to plow. When the boy complained that he could not get the straight rows his dad did, the farmer explained that the boy had to fix his eye on something distant and keep going steadily toward it. However, the boy's rows the next day were more crooked than before. The farmer asked if the boy had followed his advice, and the boy replied that he had, but the cow kept moving. We might do well to fix ourselves on one goal that will not change and keep going steadily toward it.

So what is the goal here? The word "enlightenment" refers to having a light go on that allows us to see clearly. In its capitalized form, it often refers here on earth to an age in which mankind saw new ways of thinking philosophically and of governing. But the symbolism of the word can go much farther. It can denote the state of being aware of the Spirituality that exists and is the totality of everyone and everything. It can refer to feelings of unity and oneness for all the aspects of the Universe and beyond. It might include recognizing that everyone and everything in the Universe is whole, complete, and perfect, regardless of seemingly different paths and states of being, since everything in the Universe is part of one complete Spiritual Whole. Enlightenment, then, is a vision of great peace because there is nothing to agitate or cause fear or anger or jealousy in this spiritual Oneness. It is realizing happiness in aspects of existence beyond the materialism of this world. It is the comprehension of Truth beyond what is rationally evident. It is being aware that our pathways definitely lead to a fruition of Oneness with the Divine, which puts everything else, including the material world, into perspective and makes us more calm, loving, and accepting. It is therefore all joy, for we see ourselves as part of the Presence, and nothing more can be wanted or needed as we recognize ourselves as part of the great Oneness in eternal peace and contentment.

Meditation

Meditation sets the medium through which we achieve this Enlightenment. It opens the flow of inspiration from the Spiritual that is often blocked by the constant parade of worldly thoughts from our worldly egos. It allows us to enter our inner Selves (note the capital letter) that are in constant awareness of the Spiritual, as opposed to our outer selves (note the lack of the capital) that are limited to seeing just the material part of the world around us.

We should remember that we have very few original thoughts every day. Most of what runs through our minds consists of such things as: rehashes of previous thoughts and conversations; internal stories with ourselves as the central character; remembrances of past times, with their happy elements as well as their resentments and slights; positive or negative thoughts about other people or maybe even critical comments about them to make us feel better about ourselves; worries, fears, and other destructive feelings; and the like. Have not we all on occasion dwelt on angry or negative thoughts so much that we become irritable and cranky in our dealings with others? We can do without the constant rehash of most of these thoughts, especially during our peaceful time in isolation to set our spiritual medium. To achieve Enlightenment, we need to allow a new way of seeing and sensing the totality of what is around us. We cannot solve a problem by continuing to use the methods that caused it in the first place, and so to see spiritually, we cannot continue to use the methods that keep us locked into the limited view of life that we have had so far.

Meditation can be used by ourselves or with others to put ourselves into a quiet, contemplative state without all the usual mind chatter, and then open ourselves to the flow of intuition and inspiration from our spiritual realm that takes us beyond worldly rationale. This is not easy, because the brain does not want to shut off those worldly thoughts, having us believe that they are essential parts of our personalities. But this silent state is what meditation is all about: cultivating the peaceful, spiritual plane on a new, high level of consciousness. This should be done on a regular basis because its insights need to become the essence of us even during our operations in the material world.

There are many, many methods of doing meditation. Generally, though, they entail sitting or standing comfortably in a quiet atmosphere; focusing our intentions on awareness of a higher level of consciousness than that of the material world; turning our thoughts continually to greater peace, thankfulness, and openness to the flow of spiritual inspirations that are already within us; and generally picturing ourselves as moving toward greater spiritual realizations that are actually already present within us. Some people hum or play a chant or mantra to keep the mind in focus. Others concentrate on a circle of red or gold light to do the same thing. Others drum on a small drum or listen to the sounds of drumming to set their internal rhythms. Some focus on their breathing, and picture themselves as bringing in energy from the outside with each intake, circulating it through the body, and then breathing out the spent energy on the exhale. Some relax so completely that their minds enter into an Alpha state, similar to a self-induced hypnosis, and are turned so far inward that they accept autosuggestions that allow spiritual aspects to take charge of their lives.

Regardless of the methods used, the most important thing to achieve is extending this meditative state onto our acting state, keeping the same outlook, which is now called contemplation, as we resume our daily lives. With practice, we can allow the spiritual realizations and intentions achieved in our quiet time to guide our reactions in the material world and help us actually live the lives of peace and happiness that we visualized when we were alone.

Intention

Intention sets and maintains the way we think, act, and treat ourselves, especially in enlisting spirituality to be with us in our journey of discovery. It is putting into action our decision-making and our willpower to trust, to seek, and to acquire. It is setting the course and providing the motive power to our journey toward greater and greater Enlightenment. It is an actual power in the Universe that opens the way to all accomplishment because when we open our intent to act, the elements of the Universe (which are all really one) join us in a unity of effort. Through intention, we make commitments to pursue our goals, thereby allowing spirituality and inspiration to be our constant companions. Intention also keeps us on track, helping us go right through obstacles that might arise.

As an example, if a student in a martial arts class is to break a board with bare feet, the worst way to approach this is tentatively or timidly, with the intention of not getting hurt, because the mind does not recognize a negative and will easily focus on the idea of "hurt" as the essence of the thought, which means that "hurt" may well come to pass. And by setting intention too low, there will not be enough effort made and the board will probably not even break, resulting in a damaged foot and an unbroken board. Instead, there needs to be a firm intention made to kick *through* the board to a place *behind* it in a single-minded focus, much as how a needle pierces cloth better than a finger does because all the force is concentrated on a tiny point. Our intention then guides and allows the action to take place. The foot will drive its way through the obstacle of the board to land on the intended target behind it. The board will split on the way, and there will be no injury. As we will see later, our intention does not actually *cause* the board to break, but rather allows us the power and momentum to set the stage for this to happen, which might not otherwise occur.

It is our decision, then, to set our intention either to succeed or to fail, since where we set our thoughts is where our body tends to go. Therefore, we have to be careful about where our thoughts are. We cannot waste our time in negative or critical thinking, for example, because spirituality is only positive and our negative thoughts just allow us to block it out temporarily. Intention actually aligns us with the forces of the Universe, as we shall see later, and allows us either our full fruition or our continually-blocked frustration, depending on where we choose to set it. As we look at the Higgs Field later, we will see that floating along spiritually with no action or intention to accomplish does not lead to advancement, whereas putting out intention and effort allows growth. So intention is a key attribute.

LOVE

We are constantly told that we should love each other, and that love is considered the highest attribute of a heavenly existence. But the word "love" covers such a bewildering variety of emotions that it is difficult to define it properly. Types can include: the bucolic love from afar of shepherds and shepherdesses; teenage infatuation; casual relations on a date; the development of intense caring between an engaged pair; inflamed passions of lust; the quiet, accepting love of a long-married elderly couple; the selfless, giving love of the altruist; the spiritual love referred to in the Greek word Agape; and so forth. It should be added that the passions of love can be so unstable that they can change almost instantly to hatred or something else devastating. So using the word "love" can give rise to all sorts of misunderstandings from varying definitions.

So let us use the word in capital letters as an acronym meaning: Level Of Veritable Enlightenment. The word "veritable," of course, means real or genuine. By doing the things pointed out by EMILY, we will be behaving as if we were enlightened already in this earthly existence, and therefore we will live a life of warmth, acceptance, unity, appreciation, and a cherishing of all around us. We will then realize that these are some of the attributes of an intensely spiritual life. Since we have to be sincere in order to develop spiritual insight, we will not be faking anything, but will be letting our growing spiritual insight be our true guide.

Basically, then, this LOVE consists of treating everyone and everything, including ourselves, with constant kindness, forgiveness, compassion, acceptance, appreciation, honesty, generosity, tolerance, patience, peacefulness, thoughtfulness, unselfishness, and all the other traits of a high-level consciousness. This should be done all the time, regardless of the people or things involved or the circumstances. If the ego seems to suffer when we do this, it is time to eschew those parts of the ego that protest. We will be the better for it.

Now, if that list is too long, we can concentrate on just the first two: Kindness and Forgiveness. Kindness consists of constantly regarding people and situations in pleasant, positive ways; of accepting and supporting others; of feeling empathy with others; of putting their well-being ahead of our own; of cherishing them; of being aware of any pressures or egoisms that might give us an excuse to treat them poorly; and of spreading warmth and goodwill wherever we go.

Forgiveness just takes care of the times when we slip a bit. It means releasing any damaging feelings we have against another and getting rid of them completely, developing warm feelings instead. It does not mean to pardon, for that would mean that there was a breach in the first place. We must remember that if we have something against another person, it is solely our doing, our decision, and really has nothing to with them at all. It exists because we feel the need to criticize and judge others based on our own standards, believing that our standards are better than theirs. It is really up to us to take care of the problem inside of us that has resulted in the bad feelings, and to improve our own health and well-being by not carrying around grudges.

In other words, true LOVE consists of accepting and caring about each person, plant, rock, animal, and earthly feature exactly as each is by seeing its inherent spiritual essence. It offers help in any appropriate form when requested. It puts its intention on an overall high level of consciousness, of spirituality, and of understanding so that a positive aura can be established in which beneficial changes are allowed to take place. By facilitating an increase in spiritual flow and an elevation of consciousness through greater awareness and empathy, LOVE can give birth to spiritual peace and fulfillment, allowing whatever exists now to just be, both for the other person and for ourselves. Thus we behave as if we were enlightened beings already, which is, again, what LOVE really represents: Level Of Veritable Enlightenment.

Yielding

Yielding carries forgiveness even farther and is really the culminating step in facilitating our rise to the highest levels of consciousness because it rids us of all the baggage weighing us down.

Very simply, it consists of giving up any thought of making judgments or criticisms about others, of keeping negative thoughts about them, or of considering ourselves better than they. What we can yield are such illusions as jealousies, angers, vengeances, affronts, prides, miseries, and so forth. We must give up feeling slighted or dumped on or demeaned or making ourselves the innocent victims. (Oh, how some of us enjoy our mental stories of how we have been wronged and how we plan to get our vengeance in the end!) All these are actions of the ego, which seems to get a lot of pleasure from suffering. None of these will exist when we feel the fullness of our higher consciousness. Bluntly put, barring internal chemical imbalances, we are responsible for our own feelings. If we are critical or angry or sorry for ourselves, it is because we decide to be that way. No one forces us into those reactions. They are our responsibility. Therefore, we can also decide *not* to be that way, Anger, like spirituality, is a daily decision, and that takes us back to intention again. If we really love others, we accept them just as they are, and set our intentions accordingly. It is up to us, not up to them.

What can be the result of all this? As we yield everything that might block our progress, we end our identification with worldly agitations, opinions, destructions, and uncertainties, entering instead into the peacefulness, comfort, and serenity that mark the Presence of Divinity and our Oneness with It. As we release more and more aspects of the worldly ego, we uncover more and more of our inner spiritual natures and values. We begin to see everything as beautiful, everything as peaceful, and everything as Divine. After all, there can be no uncertainty, no feelings of separation, no fear of punishment after death when we become aware of the Spirituality of everything that exists in us as being of one Unity. We can relax completely, knowing that everything is right and is everlasting, and that we are a part of it. Then we feel love, warmth, stillness, peace, and Oneness with All that Is.

These thoughts are not new; they exist already within us and just have to be recognized and allowed to function. Just as a salesman will attend a selling seminar, not to learn anything new, but to be reminded of the things he already knows and is not doing, so we can follow this inner awareness and begin to recognize and live the inner spiritual existence that will bring joy and enrichment to ourselves and to those around us. Thus EMILY can also mean EverMore I Love You!

The elements of EMILY cannot be attained in their fullness instantly. We will work on developing them side by side with our development of the elements of the Numinous Factor, so that we will evolve our cognitive awareness of the true nature of the Universe and our spiritual awareness of it at the same time, giving us a good multi-dimensional realization of what is really there.

CHAPTER TWO

● ● ● ● ● ● ● ● ●

The Factor and Limitlessness

The Numinous Factor

First, what is a "factor"? Generally, it is anything that is introduced into a situation and contributes to the outcome. When sailing a yacht or playing golf, wind is a factor that can greatly affect the path of the boat or the flight of the ball. When buying a house, the mortgage rate is a big factor in deciding what size of property to buy. In math and physics, a factor is a number that gives a result when multiplied into an equation. So a factor is an integral part of a real-life situation as well as a math problem, something that influences the result and needs to be evaluated carefully because of its effect. In fact, getting the right result depends on using the correct factors.

In like manner, there are many factors in play as people look at the Universe. Depending on their training, experience, and abilities, different people use different factors to reach their own understanding of what is out there. Some use scientific reasoning, some use pure mathematics, others use astrology, others make pictures in the stars, others plan space travel, some use religious stories they have read or been told, and each sees the Universe a little differently from everyone else. For us to understand more of the Universe around us, we need to influence our present thinking with spiritual factors that give a more complete understanding than purely logical science or star pictures can. Also, other factors might bring each of us to answers more appropriate for use in our different journeys in life than we now have.

This book is entitled The Numinous Factor. Although the word "numinous" is probably not familiar to most readers, it carries the idea of relating to the Spiritual Essence of things in non-rational ways. The word comes from the Latin "numen," thought of as a creative force, a spiritual nature that inhabits, or even is, every material entity and is part of the Creative Force. It refers to a sense of the Presence of Divinity in everything, a Presence that exists in, as, and through everything that is manifest, including what is not known to us yet. The term sees all things as being made up of a Divinity that can be felt but not logically grasped by our human thinking at the present time. Any attempt of ours to define Divinity any further leads to limiting It because our logic is weak and incapable when compared to that of Divinity. So without the Numinous, we miss the fullest understanding and interpretation of the physical things we see and measure and use. It is a concept that is very close to the idea of seeing Deity (whatever It may be named) in everything and knowing that everything is of this Deity. The Numinous thus refers to a strong, sacred, living, creative force that is the Essence of all that exists. The word is not a name, but rather a description. Giving some steps toward developing what awareness we can presently achieve of this great Spiritual Presence is the goal of this book.

LUCIE

Since we have EMILY as our guide to appreciating the Numinous spiritually, it would be good to meet a guide to approaching the Numinous in a more thinking way. This guide's name, LUCIE, is an acronym just as EMILY is, this time with her letters standing for five areas in which we can start from an accepted term in human thinking and then factor in as much or as little of a spiritual aspect as we choose to do. Here are the areas:

Limitation ⇨ Limitlessness
Uniqueness ⇨ Unity
Cause ⇨ Continuity
Intellect ⇨ Intuition
Elements ⇨Energy

We can start from the earthly factors on the left and apply the spiritual factors on the right to whatever extent we choose. By applying these spiritual Principles in a thinking way while simultaneously applying the Principles of EMILY in a spiritual way, we will have a chance to see and understand more of what is around us. LUCIE and EMILY are our two guides, each supporting and amplifying the other, and each supplying one of the two views that, combined, will give what could be likened to a three-dimensional concept of the Universe and our place in it. To remind us of the spirituality inherent in these five on the right-hand side, they will be capitalized in this book, as will be the term "Principles" when it refers to them, and the term "Numinous" throughout.

Let us now look at the first of the Five Principles of LUCIE in a little more detail and see how they all can be applied. They are not meant to be proofs of anything, but rather are keys to opening new panoramas of awareness. Their logic can go just so far by itself because our reasoning power is quite weak in comparison to the spiritual views we are seeking to uncover, and so the practice of the Five Principles of EMILY needs to go on in tandem with understanding the logic of the Five Principles of LUCIE. It would be good, then, to review and practice with EMILY for a few minutes each time we plan to delve into the thoughts of LUCIE so that the balanced view can take place.

Limitlessness

The biggest Principle is Limitlessness. Man, by his very nature, deals with limits. He is limited in the amount of time he can go without eating, drinking, or sleeping. The joints in his arms and legs keep those limbs moving in rather restricted ways. His ability to hear is nowhere near that of a dog, his ability to see in the dark nowhere near that of a cat, and he cannot breathe under water as does the fish. He constructs machines that also have limits and can break down. He tries to communicate in a variety of languages that often limit understanding. He builds bridges and buildings by carefully observing limits such as tensile strengths or the effects of gravity. He cannot drive a vehicle so fast as he might like to because of speed and safety limits. Animals, of course, are also limited, having different brains, lacking a thumb, and being guided by instincts that they do not understand. Limits are so pervasive that man even glories in his limits. Baroque music and poetic sonnets have beautiful and intricate developments within strict limits. Some musical composers try to stray into atonal music, meaning music without the limits of a fixed scale and tonality, but the results are not always pleasing to enough people, and the old limited forms generally return.

There are interesting results that occur when man decides to overcome mental and physical limits. When Jim Knaub, the Olympic-quality pole vaulter, came out of the hospital bound to a wheelchair for life because of crushed vertebrae in a traffic accident, he refused to accept the normal limits of mobility in a typical wheelchair. Still considering himself a world-class athlete, he began designing lower, faster chairs with splayed wheels for stability and hand rings nearer to the axle for speed, and could be seen racing along the streets, not the sidewalks, of Lakewood, California. However, the public, who mostly did not know what he was doing, was amazed to read that Jim was entering the Long Beach Marathon, since they had the old ideas of what wheelchairs were like. But Jim won the race, beating all the runners handily, and then proceeded to compete in the Boston Marathon, which he won a record five times, attaining the status of the greatest wheelchair athlete ever.

As another example, ever since Galileo and his telescope broke through man's limited thinking that the sky was just a dome over a flat earth, astronomers have spent a great deal of time and effort to create bigger and better telescopes, and even have found a way to mount one in space, so as to see at greater distances than before and with greater clarity, without the limitations of earth's atmosphere and rotation speed.

For us to contemplate fully the nature of The Divine Creator and all Existence, we need to overcome our limits of thinking and even the concept that there are limits. This can be difficult. For instance, trying to imagine what is outside of the Universe is just too much to handle for some people, but to deny there is anything out there is a limit, a denial of the totality of existence. Just because we cannot see something does not mean it is not there. Our eyesight or measuring instruments can show us a lot, but to assume that there is nothing outside of their limitations is to constrict our concept of Divinity, and Deity must be beyond our limits. We have never been able to see galaxies more than about fourteen billion light years away. Does this mean that the Universe is limited and that the farthest stars in it are fourteen billion light years away from us? No, a more probable answer is that the Universe itself is only fourteen billion years old, and the stars that are more than fourteen billion light years away have not been in existence long enough for their light to have reached us yet. They are quite possibly there, so we cannot limit our thinking concerning them.

In fact, astronomers have recently tripled their estimate of the number of stars in the Universe. In the Milky Way alone, the previous estimate was one hundred billion stars. Estimates now range around three hundred billion and are growing, and that is just in our own galaxy, which is just another example of how humans think that they can see everything and then set limits accordingly. Likewise, the estimated number of planets, based on the Kepler telescope data from just one tiny part of the sky, is that there are some forty or fifty billion planets going around those stars, with maybe hundreds of millions of them being located in the temperate zone of being the right distance from their star to allow life as we know it to evolve. That does not count multiple planets around a star, which are even harder to see as of yet, or planets in other zones that could support different kinds of life. But still these numbers indicate limits. Insisting on setting limiting numbers just makes us think that there is nothing else there, a concept that may block us from greater visualizations. We may have the latest numbers, but they will probably change to other limits as we discover more. After a while, we might get the idea that there are no limits, and that we have not discovered enough to assume that limits even exist. If, therefore, we deal in the concept of Limitlessness rather than that of Limits, we can identify better with the Numinous Factor.

As another example, we are accustomed to our three dimensions of width, length, and height. We can add time as our fourth dimension, and can use these four to appreciate Einstein's concept of "spacetime" as a single unit, which we will see later. However, can we assume that these four dimensions are all that exist just because we cannot see any others? Let us see how we have to remove that limitation if we are to deal with basic theories of existence such as the string theory that deals in at least eleven dimensions.

Dimensions

Here is an illustration of this problem of the limitations in dimensions. Sometimes in class, I will put six pencils of the same length on the table and challenge the students to make four equilateral triangles with them. Well, they usually lay out one triangle with three of the pencils, then put two more to make a second triangle using one side of the first, and are then perplexed on how to make the remaining two triangles with only one pencil. When they are stumped, I point out that they are visualizing in only two dimensions, and that they need to free themselves from that limitation. I make the first triangle, and then lay the other pencils across it in a three-dimensional way, producing four triangles. They are of different sizes, of course, since the bottom pencils are at different distances from the apex, but are all equilateral, meaning that the sides of each are all the same length. The students find themselves jolted from the two-dimensional limit that they created for themselves automatically. But the illustration does not stop there.

The students then usually protest that they thought I meant that all the sides of all the triangles had to be the same length. I promptly agree to that, and challenge them to do it that way. Again, they fail, even though they are trying three-dimensional ways to do it, such as piling up three pencils along one side. I then show them that they are not thinking far enough out into the three dimensions. Again, I lay out the base triangle. I then take the other three pencils and stand them up, placing the eraser of each at one of the angles of the first triangle while holding all the points together over the center. Thus we have one triangle lying flat, and three others standing up, each using one side of the flat one, and all having their sides the same length. The students quickly get the idea of ridding themselves of dimensional limitations. In like manner, the more we rid ourselves of any concept of limits, the more able we are to see the Numinous in everything.

We remember that this is why we use the term "Numinous" in the first place, rather than one of the religious names for Deity. As soon as we say one of those names, the reader will automatically apply the limitations of past thinking or teachings to that name, thereby installing a limited view spiritually. We do not use the Numinous out of disrespect to any of the current Names of Deity, but to free ourselves from past limitations of definitions and expand ourselves to the greater idea of the limitless Presence of the Divine in everything that exists, whether seen or unseen, unfettered by human-induced constrictions and definitions. The concept of limitlessness, then, is not a doctrine or dogma, but rather a release from confining doctrines that hamper our seeing the greater picture due to our self-imposed structure of limits.

Let us look at three words that have been used many times to describe Deity over the centuries of human endeavor and see how they can help release us from limits. Supposedly, these three concepts are included in generally-accepted opinions of the nature of the Divine, in the human view, but they are usually applied in a limited sense due to mankind's confining concepts. Let us look at them here, not to give a personality or a definition to the Divine, but rather to release the concept of the Divine from its human confinement. The three concepts are: Omniscience, Omnipotence, and Omnipresence. Once we see the infinite natures of these terms, we can form them into a unity that we can call the Omniconstant.

Omniscience

Omniscience means "all-knowing," and refers to the fact that the Numinous must know everything in order to be responsible for every aspect of the Universe. In fact, reflection may show that the Numinous must be the *Author* of all knowledge, or else a situation could arise where someone knew something before the Numinous did, and that would seem to be an impossibility. It is vital that the Numinous be infinite in knowledge. Humans keep discovering more and more about electricity, for example, but the Numinous had to know everything about it throughout all time since electricity is apparently present in its entirety throughout Creation.

Omniscience is huge and complex. It includes knowing all facts relating to everything throughout the Universe, whether in material form or not, from the actions of the largest galaxies to detailed operations of a subatomic world so small that we humans can hardly comprehend it. All of this has to remain in balance with tiny tolerances and never vary throughout the ages. Omniscience also involves keeping track of all matter in all its stages of development, of anti-matter, and of all the dark energies that humans do not, as yet, comprehend at all. And it means knowing all thoughts and mental images that have ever been had by any and all living, thinking beings on this planet or on any other, which is a staggering complexity in itself.

But Omniscience goes even farther than this enormous view. It can be sensed that there can be no thought that is not actually of the Numinous. Each thought can be seen as part and parcel of the Infinite. When people are trying to find their Supreme Being, they miss the point that the very thoughts with which they are searching are of the Spiritual Realm Itself. And since every action starts in a thought, all actions are therefore of the Numinous. Thus there is nothing that we do or say or experience that is not spiritual. This can be a new and extraordinary concept for some people, but it will become more clear and evident when we discuss Omnipresence, wherein the Numinous may be sensed as being everywhere and in everything. A fish does not ask what water is because he is in it. It is the medium through which he moves and lives and receives life-giving elements. He cannot conceive of life outside of it, and actually does not even know it is there. (Given the five-second attention span of a fish, he would forget it anyway.) Likewise, we humans live mentally in a medium, an atmosphere, a life-giving source that is Numinous, but we do not see or sense it but, instead, go around looking for it as being separate from us when we are in it all the time. The Numinous is all there is, and all of our thinking, sensing, and perceiving is a part of It.

This brings us to the question of how the Numinous could be the author of thoughts considered to be evil or wicked. Well, these last two words have been defined in many different ways by many different peoples and sects without a universal consensus. The concept of "evil" is, therefore, a product of human judgment, and is actually a religious term, to be defined by each religious group. Since there is no universally-accepted definition of the term, what is considered evil by one group is perfectly acceptable to another. What lists of definitions do exist seem to be vague and have many interpretations, so their use is up to each individual. A thermometer does not measure whether something is too hot or too cold, but just shows temperatures on a sliding scale. Anything else is a human judgment. Spirituality just is, and deals with things that just are.

We humans might say, in general, that violent, destructive thoughts are bad while loving, constructive thoughts are good, which seems to match how higher spirituality is said to bring peace and happiness instead of warfare, anger and sorrow. This sounds reasonable, but when we look closely at the Universe, it seems to be built to a great degree on what we call violence. For example, scientists think that the Universe started with a gigantic explosion with heat so intense that regular atomic activity was impossible. Even now, our sun is wracked by explosions. Stars passing by other stars violently strip off materials that they attract to themselves. Perhaps we need to hold off making judgments and definitions about good and bad until we understand a little more.

Actually, when stars strip off material from other stars, they use this material to build solar systems, and constructive elements such as oxygen probably came to this planet through just such a violent action. Meteors and other space debris crash into other bodies with great temporary destruction, but help them grow in the long run. Destructive volcanoes here on earth fertilize fields with fresh and balanced minerals from the interior of the earth. Is destruction bad when it leads to growth? This is a personal judgment call in each situation. We would really be upset if a passing meteor were to crash into us with great destruction, but volcanoes and meteors are normal parts of the operation of the Universe. On the other hand, even such a simple action as heating soup for dinner causes great agitations of particles as they crash into each other producing elevated temperatures in the soup, and yet we accept this violence as normal. So, again, the question of good and evil in violence is actually a human judgmental problem and has little to do with our study here.

Let us take another example. It is interesting to contemplate that disease is also a part of the Numinous. Divinity knows the human body and its weakness to bacteria, but bacteria are part of the totality of creation (for millions of years the only life existing on this planet consisted of bacteria) and are still allowed to invade human bodies as part of the material life. Some bacteria are benign and necessary for life, other types cause tissue trauma. So are the diseases that might result from bacterial invasions bad or just normal functioning? When bacteria are necessary for proper bodily growth and proper functioning, such as breaking down our food or wood from fallen logs in the forest so that nourishment and new growth can occur, are they evil? It could be said that our job as intelligent beings is to improve these situations, but sometimes our meddling makes things worse, such as the overuse or incomplete use of antibiotics that has resulted in the creation of Golden Staph strains that cannot be stopped by any known medication. We think about peoples who lived long ago and suffered and died from things that we cure routinely today and ask ourselves: Were they any less in the Numinous? What is the true function of a healing consciousness? We will get further into such questions later, but suffice it to say now that simple, pat answers from our established thought patterns do not always resolve problems, and we need to be sensitive to thoughts and ideas and concepts that may seem strange to us presently, but which are still a part of the Numinous since the Numinous is all knowledge.

Omnipotence

This term means that the Numinous must be all-powerful. We are talking about having *all* of the power, not just some of it. Probably, it would be easier to think of the Numinous as *being* all of the power. This is in opposition to some writings that picture the Supreme Being as needing the help of other beings in the fight against the powers of Evil, or being limited in the ability to create or to control the objects created. Well, we already saw the problems inherent in defining Evil, but maybe it would make things easier if we saw the Power of the Numinous as being a field of strength that is quiet, self-sustaining, insurmountable, and everlasting, not needing to do anything because its strength is absolute and its presence is everywhere. With Power, nothing really happens. Everything just exists within its field. Gravity just is and things operate within it. As we grow to see Limitlessness, then, we grow to realize that what we call good or evil or health or sickness are just relative terms on a sliding scale and are all part of the Numinous, the only Power in the Universe. There is a limitation built into the idea that sickness and poverty are errors that need to be corrected, and in the idea that our healing actions are always necessary to restore a condition to where we think it ought to be. Such a definition is merely an outgrowth of our imperfect human judgment. Since everything is the Numinous, everything is just as it should be already because the Numinous is all there is. It is our human outlooks that seem to see problems and lacks.

Now, using healing actions to set up a condition that we may feel to be beneficial according to our human judgment is a choice that we are allowed to make in our freedom of operation, but to assume that the condition we try to correct is wrong or bad is to deny the oneness of everything in the Numinous. There is no ability that the Numinous does not have, and so there is no power of which the Numinous is not the Source and the Totality. Just like thoughts, every bit of action we take, or strength that we exert in our small ways is part of It. All creation, both of things seen by us and those unseen, is Numinous.

We ourselves do not create anything. A doctor knows that he does not heal anyone. He can set up the proper field and conditions for a change of state, but it is still the Numinous that does the changing. There is a delicate balance in such activities. For example, using certain drugs to block heart arrhythmias can lead to a dangerously low pulse rate. In such a case the cure may be worse than the original problem. This may lead us to ponder our use of the word "heal" and how we think that we must step in and "correct" a condition that seems to us to be in error. The Numinous does not need a bailout.

All the power to keep the smallest subatomic entities as well as the largest galaxies in proper balance as they develop is of the Numinous. All the power to create anything that exists in this Universe and in other universes is of It. This is a limitless concept. The numinous cannot just have some of the power or there would be things outside of It that could not be done. There can be contrasts, to our human perception, but there can be no opposition. There can be no alternates in an Absolute. For example, centrifugal force, or maybe Newton's first law, tries to get planets to fly off into space at their great orbit speeds, whereas gravity is what keeps them circling their sun. There is no opposition in this. If the Numinous had only part of the power, that balance would not be effective and everything would fly apart, so the balance is not opposition but apposition, the placing of things in juxtaposition. It is all part of the Unity that we will see later. The Numinous also has power over the dark matter, the dark energy, the black holes, and other phenomena of which we have only the barest knowledge. In fact, our knowledge is so terribly limited that we are in no position to define the Supreme Being in any way. The power of the Numinous is complete and limitless, and we just share in a tiny bit of it.

Omnipresence

Omnipresence is another word that has to be used in its limitless sense. This can be the toughest concept of the Numinous for humans to grasp, but is basic for the proper assimilation of the Factor. The term means that the Numinous must be present everywhere, not only throughout space, but in every atom, molecule, rock, tree, flower, person, meteor, planet, moon, star, galaxy, and universe that exists or ever will exist, and must be in Its completeness everywhere, not partially. We are talking about the Numinous' actually being the soul and fabric of everything. Now, there are those who will laugh at this, thinking that it is like the ancients who worshipped the sun, the rain, the lightening, or various animals, saying that they were individual gods. It is not that. It is seeing Spirituality as the basis of everything that exists anywhere.

Seeing Omnipresence means recognizing the Oneness of the Numinous with all creation, being the fabric and completeness of everything. If there is no thought that is not the Numinous, nor power separate from It, then there can be no place without the Numinous' Presence for that power or those thoughts to operate. If there is Oneness, it must be complete. There can be no place to which the Numinous only sends a representative, because the Numinous must have complete power in every place, a totality. Throughout recorded human history, there have been people and even religious beliefs that have identified with the earth, with nature, with the oneness of everything as being part of the Oneness of the Numinous with all of Creation. This is actually an advanced concept and is central to understanding the totality of the Universe and our place in it. As a side note, however, too often, people assume a "tick-tock" theory, in which some Deity did create the Universe, but then wound it up and left it to operate independently while He went off elsewhere to do other things. There is also the tribal chieftain concept of Deity, which assumes all sorts of limitations of power, possession of human traits, the concept that some people are rewarded for "good" behavior while others are punished for "bad" behavior (whatever those terms may mean), and so forth. These and other limiting views miss the point completely: Oneness and Totality mean just that, and infinite limitlessness is present in its completeness in the Numinous, free from human restrictions and narrow views.

Now, an interesting point opens up here. Over the generations, man has had the idea that he is down here on earth while Deity is up in the heavens. Man has also had the idea that he was made as an imperfect being and must find a way to overcome his imperfections to be able to rise and rejoin this Deity in Heaven and live there in happiness for the rest of the eternities. If he fails, he will suffer in some place of torment forever. This concept is called "duality," and is one of the most prevalent underlying doctrines in various belief systems and one of the most difficult to overcome in the gaining of spiritual awareness. So let us put it bluntly: Acceptance of the concept that Deity is in, as, and through everything that exists gets rid of the concept of duality. There can be no idea of separation when the basic essence of man is the Numinous in the first place.

So we have seen the concept that the Numinous is present in every thought that man has and in every action that he takes because the Numinous is the Essence of them all, and now we see that the Numinous is actually present in everything that exists, both seen and unseen. There is no duality. Therefore, man cannot be evil because Spirituality is in him and in everything else, which means that the idea of "evil" is a human judgment and is of shaky validity. It is a human definition, and there are so many interpretations of the word that there is no one standard on the whole earth that can be used to judge mankind. Most efforts to do so seem to be man-made, and come from the same type of limited thinking as was in those who forced Galileo to renounce his claim that the earth was not the center of the Universe even when he could clearly see moons orbiting other planets as he peered through his telescope. Furthermore, since Spirituality is in and as everyone, it is hard to see how anyone is going to be "lost" and spend the eternities in some place of suffering. Everyone is on an individual path, but all paths must lead back to Oneness after the earthly time is over because Oneness is all there is ultimately. There is no duality of heaven and hell, no duality of saved and lost, no duality of right and wrong. These are human definitions and they ignore the Omnipresence and Oneness of the Numinous.

However, thoughts and actions do have consequences or "karma," and when we choose something, we are also choosing its consequences. To call these "evil" or "good" is, again, human judgment, but there are still consequences, some of which may not be immediately apparent. Doing drugs may give a temporary high, but there are long-term consequences to health and mentality. The characteristics of LOVE in EMILY can lead to consequences for us and for others when we practice them. They may seem to us to be the characteristics of a higher spiritual life from the intuitions we may receive in our meditations, but to call them "good" can be a misnomer to the person who has a different personal viewpoint. However, each person might note carefully if their viewpoints go against the principle of Oneness of everything.

Oneness, then, means lack of separateness or duality, and we might see ourselves as all one in the Numinous. The rock, the earth, the human, the animal, the tree, the plant, and the star all are one in Creation, and each has a role to play. Give some thought to the concept that an atom is an atom. Look at your hand and contemplate that the carbon atoms in it came from the center of a massive star somewhere that exploded, scattering the heavier elements produced in its core. These elements were picked up by another star and wound up as part of this earth and, therefore, part of your hand. The hydrogen atoms in our bodies are the same as those in the sun or in another planet or in the body of another living being. An electron is an electron; they are all the same. People are really all the same, basically. Do you remember the story of a lull in the gunfire in the forward lines of World War I on Christmas Eve? In the comparative silence, a German in the forward trenches began singing "Stille Nacht" and soon an Allied soldier in his forward trench a short distance away joined in, singing "Silent Night" in English. More voices joined in, and when they had sung several carols together, they began coming out of their trenches to visit, shake hands, wish the enemy soldiers a Merry Christmas, and to swap candy bars and cigarettes as presents. They were all one at heart. Then the magical moment was over, and they were ordered back to the trenches to try to kill each other once more in a war set up by political leaders dealing in duality.

So the only "enemies" we have are just other people following their own equally valid paths according to their own beliefs. If we judge or criticize anyone or have problems in getting along with others, we should remember the principle of "Yielding" in EMILY and know that how we react to these situations is strictly our decision, showing where we are on our path to spiritual awareness. People tend to see what they are looking for, as we saw in the speaker with the two pictures. If someone does not like us, that has nothing to do with us; it is just how they see things according to their own standards, which are not our standards. So we do not have to be concerned with their views. People will see the characteristics that they choose to see or have been programmed to see, and that is where a different view of the Numinous might break up this prior programming and allow a fresh view. In the absence of separatist dogma, we should sense that the Numinous is all there is, and if something were not right, it would have changed by now. And so instead of finding fault or indulging in hatreds, we can look for the Spiritual Oneness, if that is how we choose to follow our path. That is our decision. Everyone and everything is important just because it is, because it exists. It was brought forth in this way at this time. Everything is the way it is because it is part of the Spiritual Universe. A twisted tree is not a deformed tree, but rather is a perfect twisted tree. It is our human judgment that sees something deformed or wrong. We can find more happiness in appreciating the tree for what it is than for finding fault just because it is not what we would like it to be. We, our spouses, our business associates, our acquaintances, and our friends, can all be much happier if we look for the spiritual in each other and just appreciate any differences that might exist as being part of the infinite creativity of the Numinous.

So we have Omniscience, Omnipotence, and Omnipresence. These three suggest many areas of Spiritual Perfection, and will be treated as a single Constant that applies to any consideration of the Numinous, just like a mathematical constant applies to an equation. This Constant can be referred to as the Omni constant, and can be abbreviated 3O or, of even more symbolism, 3OM. By a happy turn of semantics, those who use the sound "OM" as a mantra or chant to refer to Deity in their meditations can hear that in the abbreviation.

CHAPTER THREE

· · · · · · · ·

Unity and Continuity

The Ego

The second Principle of LUCIE takes us from Uniqueness to Unity. To start, let us talk about the ego. The ego can be defined as the vision that we carry of ourselves, our feeling of identity, and the set of ways in which we act and react. It is related to our personality, which is the list of characteristics that we (and others) say that we have. There are two problems with personalities: in the first place, other people are generally wrong in what they think about us, in part because they only see a little of us, and in part because they are coming from their own limitations and biases that keep them from seeing objectively; and in the second place, we are often wrong about ourselves, mostly from either pride or low self esteem, and also from mixing the character traits that we seem to have with those that we would like to have. So people are generally wrong about themselves and about everyone else. The ego, however, takes the traits that we like to think that we have, combines them with those that we have been told that we have since we were very young by parents, teachers, siblings, church people, and even strangers, and makes this combination our "self," our personal identity. There can be times when we might judge this a plus, such as when we have family members who believe in us and keep encouraging us to achieve at high levels, and we can judge it a minus when we are told by others that we are stupid or troublemakers. We tend to accept these criteria without question. We note that we recognize the strengths and weaknesses of our physical identities, and go to great lengths to keep looking good on the outside. But although we also may recognize what growth we need on the inside, we still mix what we want to be with what others say that we are, and the result is often a big fake. However, the ego does not care, and goes on to establish this "person" over the years as an entity separate and distinct from everyone and everything else, and therein lies the problem.

Now, we generally presume that everything has a purpose because the Supreme Power has continued the system that we see. It is not up to us to question: "Why?" There are apparently some issues that need to be handled with the spiritual element clothed in a physical body. All this is a part of the normal Creativity and Continuity of the Universe. Yet, the Universe is not static. It expands and changes constantly, as we shall soon see, and so we humans change and grow in body, mind, personality, and spirituality. We see this easily in the first three areas, but with spirituality, we sometimes remain constrained by limitations that we do not even recognize since they have been built into us from our early youth. So, just as some animals need to grow physically by shedding their skins or by breaking open the shells around their bodies or by doing a metamorphosis into completely new identities, perhaps we ourselves need to break open or shed something in order to free ourselves for spiritual growth.

The problem is that the ego sets itself as an identity that *is separate from everyone else.* This is one of our biggest limitations. We feel that we are different from other people; that we are better than some and worse than others; and that we are alone without anyone to really understand us. The ego fights fiercely to maintain this separate identity, and to keep us from assimilating any other. It sets up an entity so strongly independent that it insists on being allowed to continue to exist even after the body and brain die. Some people loosely use the term "at one with God," but still mean a close but separate physical relationship between two independent beings, much like giving a hug rather than actually blending with the other person.

What is wrong with this picture? Well, it destroys the principle of Oneness, it is duality to the max, it puts walls between us and other people, it keeps us from identifying ourselves with spiritual Continuity, it limits us to fixed ways of thinking and doing, and it often leads to antagonism with and disparagement of others. It is the opposite of unity. It actually separates us from the Deity we wish to embrace, and therefore creates tension because of the human desire for completeness, which many people feel comes from returning to Heaven as they conceive of it, or fulfilling life's journey in the Presence of Divinity. What is more, the ego's separatism denies the fundamental truth of who we really are underneath all this worldly exterior and public persona. Actually, Limitlessness is already within us! All we have to do is realize it. To see how this works, we have to look at the concept of "Self" as compared to that of the "self."

Self and self

The "self," with a little "s," is the ego-based personality that is more fiction than fact and is terribly limited. It is the symbol of separation and human weakness. If we look past it, there is a part of man's make-up that desires and can comprehend a spiritual relationship, and this part can be called the "Self," with a capital "S." This is our spiritual side, the part that feels such emotions as: oneness rather than division; love and good will rather than selfishness or putting the other down; sharing rather than greed; happiness at the success of others rather than envy; appreciating peacefulness and calmness rather than the agitations of an ego that is struggling against the world.

The Self, then, is the part of us in communion with spirituality and, indeed, actually seems to be in and as the Spiritual Presence whenever we set our intentions to that end, such as in meditation or in living a benevolent existence. The self deals in force to get what it wants, such as compelling, commanding, punishing, and demanding. The Self deals in what could be called positive power, meaning the still, silent, spiritual existence that gives energy rather than takes it away; is calm, content, confident, and immovable; that just exists with the All in All. The Self is aware that the only real peace is that of the domain of the Numinous, at the highest levels of spirituality, and therefore it remains open to that Oneness.

What, then, is the unity we can feel when we focus on the Self and its communion with the Numinous? Let us look again at an atom for an example. As we have seen, an atom of hydrogen is like every other atom of hydrogen, whether it is in the cool water we have on earth or in the intensely hot fusion process at the center of our sun. The hydrogen in our bodies is the same as that in everyone else's body, in the trees and animals around us, and even in the bodies of similar beings on other planets. The same goes for the other elements in our bodies and we will see later how they are all just energy anyway, and energy is energy. Therefore, we are all one physically because we are made of the same stuff. We should therefore suspect that we are all One spiritually as well.

Faced with this, we might say, in order to maintain our individuality, that our chemicals may be the same, but we people are certainly different from the animals and the trees since they are obviously different physically from us and do not have the capabilities that we do. The answer to that goes beyond the abilities of animals to hear and smell better than humans do, and for trees to lift tons of water, which humans cannot do unaided. It goes to the fact that everything and everyone is the Numinous, and each has a purpose. We cannot say that one entity is better than another. If trees did not take in carbon dioxide and give off oxygen, the free oxygen needed by animals and humans would soon be depleted and we would all die. This has been master-designed to be in balance, and all of it is valuable and all of it is of the Numinous. Therefore, we embrace the tree, we rejoice in the flowering success of the plant, we marvel at the vast inherent potential energy of a simple rock, we regard with awe the massive galaxies, and we remember that everything we have here, such as carbon, is dependent on what has already happened out in space, as we saw earlier. Everything is one in Unity.

"Well," you might then say, "at least I know I am different from that other person because my face and body are different and I think differently." The answer to that is no, not really. Our bodies have some physical differences due to the infinite ways of creating a human being, just as snowflakes all have different geometric patterns, but are all seen as snowflakes, and human bodies are all pretty much the same. Most of your thoughts are the same as theirs. Your emotions and feelings are mostly the same as theirs. The things that seem to be different are from human judgments, and are still a part of Unity because the Oneness of Divinity is not made up of identical clones, but of a wide variety of people that seem to be different as a result of the infinite variety of Creativity. As an example, think of a portrait of President Lincoln made up of tiny dots of varying shades of white, black and grey. They go together to make up a portrait of a great man, but on close examination, the dots are found to be detailed pictures related to him in their own right, their general shadings adding to the shadings of the presidential portrait. Likewise, all the infinite varieties of people, animals and other entities of this planet all go together to make up the Unity of the Numinous as expressed here. The more we look for unity and togetherness, the more we will see that we are all one in the Numinous, and that the physical is merely a fleeting manifestation of the vastness of the One. All is spiritual in the totality of Oneness that is itself completely spiritual.

Let us look more closely at that. If the Divine Creator is One with all creation, as "Omnipresent" means, and is the Source of all the energy and creative power within everything, as "Omnipotent" means, and has knowledge of every thought and physical manifestation, as "Omniscient" means, then everything is One in the Numinous and therefore everything contains everything else within itself since the Numinous is the basis of it all. There is no separation, as we think there is. There are no individual "things," as physics indicates, nor individual "people," as sociology indicates, nor any separate religions, philosophies, or emotions. This all may seem to be impossible, but we note that, since we see quantum physics rules of operation that are quite different from those in our everyday Newtonian world, we should constantly use Limitlessness and not restrict ourselves to expecting all truth to lie in our present spheres of limited awareness. The more we apply the Numinous Factor, the more we will see this Oneness, and we will have many opportunities to do this later on.

This, then, needs to be a part of the Spiritual Factor: the concept of seeing the Unity of everything in the Universe, knowing that everything is actually spiritual and arises from that spirituality. This takes us to the next Principle, that of going from Cause to Continuity.

Causes

We seem to live in a world of causes, as seen through the understandings of our egos. These causes seem to be quite logical, as in the view that the cause of a table lamp's being broken is the cat's tipping it over. Strings of causes can be endless, such as the reason for the car's being dented is that another car hit it, and the cause of that was the other driver's distraction while fiddling with the radio, and the cause of that was someone else's having changed the station previously, and the cause of that was the teenager's having used the car instead of his bicycle, and on it goes. We automatically deal in causes, and even in this book, the term "because" is used quite a bit in the effort to explain things since that is the way that people are accustomed to thinking.

However, cause is a judgment call that is often wrong. If a man is seen staggering out of a bar, it could easily be assumed that he has been drinking. However, the man could have difficulty walking and just stopped in to use the phone to call a cab, but his reputation can be damaged if quick assumptions are made. Human judgments come from people with limited perspectives, little knowledge, and biased viewpoints wherein they see what they want to see, or have a selective power to focus on one aspect of something while ignoring other aspects, or need to debase others in order to raise themselves in everyone's eyes, or any of a long list of limitations, all of them coupled with the human propensity to judge and the human need to be right. To them, these "causes" are facts, but no one on earth really sees facts. Everyone sees personal opinions from limited viewpoints and large biases. Everything people see has been filtered through their interpretations before reaching their awareness.

Real causes would be difficult to see anyway. Why a person might like a particular sport or a certain kind of music could be hidden so deeply in their psyche or their past or their non-rational emotions that even they do not know the reason for it. Since this is so, how could others of much more limited access to the facts know it? We can surmise a lot *about* something, but to know it well, we have to *be* it, and even then, we would have trouble understanding all of the factors that could be considered causes.

We could say that there is a Cause to Creativity Itself that we just do not see yet, and the only Entity big enough would be what is often called First Cause or Deity. This just puts us into the folly of trying to find Deity's Cause from our human limitations. It is better to see the constant Omnipresence of the Numinous in and as everything, functioning as the animating Spiritual dimension, and forget about the need to find a Cause. Likewise, we could try to go back to the beginning of a solar system and say that a passing star caused material to be stripped away from one galaxy and then be used to form another galaxy, but then we are faced with where the star and the material to strip away came from in the first place and why they were at that location in the second place. Trying to find causes is an endless task, and they are still just opinions from our limited and biased perspectives.

So it is better to see everything as just arising from the Numinous, a constant on-going vitality in which everything has its own role and its own existence as part of the living Omnipresence of the Numinous. When everything is in Unity, it is all one body and it just is the way it is. We may see a time lag as seeming to have things linked in a chain with each one causing a subsequent one. But time is a warp in space, as Einstein realized, and all things are actually in an Eternal Present, so there is no cause. When things are seen this way, the effort to find causes just detracts from spirituality and adds to duality, trying to show that causes are separate from or just used by Deity in the Creative process. So nothing is caused, but rather just arises out of the continuing Creativity that is the nature of the Numinous. This puts the emphasis right where it should be.

Continuity

Rather than use the terms "Creation" or "Continuing Creativity," then, it might be better to identify this on-going nature of the Numinous as "Continuity." The idea of creation implies bringing something out of nothing. In the Book of Genesis in the Bible, the Hebrew word translated into English as "created" really means "organized." This is a much better word. The materials in the Universe are all present and are constantly re-organized into different manifestations in a ceaseless, unified succession as part of the Numinous. There is no cause, since it all is of the essence of the Numinous. It is timeless and is all happening simultaneously. Since, as we just saw, it is only our human need to see things in a linear fashion that creates the illusions of time and succession when time really is a warp or bending of the space fabric, then all is really ongoing and uninterrupted, a grand continuity. As we find out more about the operations of the Universe from a spiritual viewpoint, we will see that everything is Numinous, and within this, there is constant recycling, such as particles in the electromagnetic spectrum springing into life and then sinking back, just to do it again. This is Continuity. These cycles exist at all the levels of nature, and form a continuity of recycling that can extend even to other universes. We know that energy cannot be created or destroyed, so it must be constantly recycled, and since energy is really all there is in the Universe, as we shall see later, there is no individual creativity but only continuity and re-organization.

However, we do seem to see sequences in our earthly viewpoints, and it is easy to confuse "sequence" with "cause." Sequence refers to the order in which things occur, saying nothing concerning what brought them about. One thing just appears to follow another in a linear succession. Now, we have just seen that the appearance of each comes from the overall evolvement of the Universe and the propensity of things to manifest themselves in a continuum. There seems to be a sequential order, to be sure, but only when seen from our limited perspective. We may see one car after another coming around a curve in the road, but when seen from above, all the cars are there at once and all moving together as a whole, so there is not really a sequence. Neither is there one cause, since we do not know the reason each driver has for being there. As we stumble across the event, we just see that it exists as a whole in front of us.

In physics, causes do seem to be more obvious, such as a planet's being discovered because it makes another planet wobble slightly in its orbit, or the particle nature of light leading scientists to calculate how much it would bend around the moon in an eclipse and experiments show that it does. Such successes might make scientists confident that, in time and with enough knowledge, they could predict anything, even black holes or the occurrence of an earthquake in Southern California. But a problem exists with all this: It takes away the oneness aspect that each thing or event has from being a part of All that Is, of the Totality of Continuity, having its own identity within the Whole. Assuming that it comes into existence solely through being caused by something else puts the creative essence on the something else, and pushes the true continuous nature of the Numinous into the background. The wobbling of a planet is just an individual aspect of the Whole, an aspect of the ongoing process. Our seeing the concept that it is not caused, but just is as part of the Totality, represents a fundamental leap in identifying with the Numinous.

The Oneness of Continuity

Therefore, we should look at factoring in the concept that nothing has a cause. Everything just is as part of the infinite number of manifestations of the Numinous. Instead of looking for causes, we can accept the concepts of beingness, renewal, and change. The scientist will do a great job in his realm of thought about cause, and will answer a great many questions about how physical processes and manifestations affect others, but something is always lacking even in the best scientific explanation since everything really just arises in its own unique aspect of being part of the Oneness. This is not dogma, but is just what can be seen if we back off far enough from our earthly dogmas and doctrines to see the limitless picture. This is best done in a meditative state that allows intuitions and inspirations to flow.

Such concepts as the lack of cause require their own medium of contemplation for them to be understood properly, namely the spiritual or numinous medium rather than the medium of earthly logic. As we shall see in the next chapter, earthly thinking is great so far as it goes, but opening ourselves to Intuitions that come from outside our logical reasoning can lead to greater understanding than the type of thinking limited by lack of knowledge and by narrow viewpoints.

Also, to dwell on causes is to use them to predict, and to predict is to assume the mind of a Master Creator. Yes, we seem to do it all the time here in this physical world. But even if we seem to have successes, it could be that only in our present three dimensions or frame of spacetime certain things appear to happen. We do not know all the dimensions or ramifications of the overall Creative process of the Universe. The true natures of things could be radically different in other venues, in other locations in space. As a simple example, we know of three different systems of physics here on earth: Newtonian physics, which deals with how things seem to be here

39

around us; Einsteinian physics which has to do with the hugeness of space and with happenings in the whole Universe; and quantum physics, which deals with the subatomic world. These three systems are not compatible, so that laws and equations that work well in one system do not work in another, and some are set to remain enshrouded in mystery forever. So our knowledge of causes is quite limited. Also, if we think we see causes in one system, they are not necessarily causes in another. We think we see cause and effect work in this Newtonian world, but the wave of possibilities for each event in the quantum world can lead to many possible results for the same one, all of which could happen. So it is safer to see everything as part of a continuing Continuity.

It could be argued that this would lead to every person's getting a different version of the truth. Precisely. Just as people differ in their opinions of what is the best music or food or hobby, there is room for a variety of outcomes of any impending event, and so there is no one cause for any one outcome. The Numinous is made up of an infinite number of different entities. We remember how the dots making up the picture of President Lincoln are themselves individual scenes, going together to make one great portrait. Observers of physical happenings are all on different paths of life, as we will see later, and so all will see different "causes" and "results." One could say that, if enough scientists measure something and get the same result, this shows true cause and effect, but how many is enough if they are all operating from the same plane of understanding? As the saying goes, you cannot solve a problem by using the same methods that caused it in the first place. For example, a truck once got stuck in an underpass in Los Angeles, and all of the normal efforts of the work crews with crowbars, pneumatic hammers, and pulling tractors trying to get it back out were put at naught by a little boy looking on who suggested that they just let some air out of the tires. Many different researchers might wind up getting the same result, but it really could be because they were all using the same tools.

So here is the crux of the matter: If we assume that "A" causes "B," then we are removing "B" from being its own entity, with its own completeness and self-existence. And we are giving "A" a force that it seems to have only when seen through our limited perspective. Instead, through Continuity, "A" is in motion and "B" is in motion, and both are part of the Continuity of the Whole and arise from it. Since "A" arises from the Continuity, "B" must also arise from the same Continuity in its own essence. Nothing causes anything, and everything just results from the Continuity of existence. Accepting this point is a vital key to seeing the Numinous.

Since our human thinking can lead us to misunderstand the Universe, with the resultant difficulty of seeing the Numinous, let us look at another way of receiving and processing information.

CHAPTER FOUR

• • • • • • • • •

Intuition and Energy

Intellect

The fourth Principle will take us from using intellect for understanding our surroundings to using Intuition. We are, of course, proud of being intelligent beings. Each of us has a large brain with a large cerebellum and frontal lobe wherein we process millions of thoughts every day. On our left side, we carry our logical processes that lead to conclusions, and on the right, we experience beauty and emotions that lead to great pleasure and artistry. We often enjoy using these brains to solve problems, such as crossword puzzles or math problems, and know that we increase our neuron pathways and thus out ability to think as we continue to do these things. We put so much emphasis on the brain that we forget that intelligence exists throughout the body such as how decisions are made and carried out even at the cell level and without direct input from the brain itself.

After all, our brains are fine processing centers, capable of making associations and seeing patterns in data that give conclusions, but they are little more than that. Most of the thoughts in them are repetitions of earlier thoughts, or routine sequences that we have done many times before or inputs that come from the material world. We have very few original thoughts every day, and even the ones that seem to be new are usually the same old ones using different data in the cycle. And many of our thinking sequences are based on aspects of the physical world around us along with the influences of people and things that we experience. They are tied to our "self," the personality and the ego that we like to think defines our essence, as we saw in our look at uniqueness.

But it can be argued that our real "Self" is in tune with Spirituality and is not dependent on our usual thoughts, which often have to do with earthly or limiting things such as angers, jealousies, lack of understanding, and the like. When we have unlimited, lofty thoughts, such as those of serene beauty, warm oneness with others, or insights into eternal truths, it is not clear how much of this is from the functioning of the brain and how much comes from our reception of outside influences or inspirations. Possibly most of the thoughts that we consider to be original actually come from spiritual intuition rather than from logical deduction since, as we have just seen, none of us deals in "facts," but only in narrow perspectives. Even scientists cannot know facts since they, as well as we, receive only limited information in the first place, with everything filtered through our layers of accumulated responses, limited knowledge, and biased thinking in the second place. We may think we are doing a factual analysis of data, but even with proper measurement technology, we lack many of the aspects of physical phenomena, and we also process things in a limited, biased atmosphere, often not even being aware of what vision we lack. So we have to go beyond "facts" to see real truths, and maybe go to those outside influences to see the roles that they play in our thinking. Input from outside influences is often called "inspiration" or "intuition."

Intuition

Intuition refers to achieving knowledge directly, as from an outside source, without human logic or maybe even knowledge. It can be thought of as mental creativity in an earthly sense with motivation to higher spirituality, but the line between the earthly and the spiritual is often blurred. Do we receive awareness of beauty through the intellect, or through spiritual revelation? Do we invent through inspiration or perspiration? Realizing the answer to this is easier than it first seems to be when we remember that all information we receive comes from the Numinous anyway because of Omniscience. There is no secular knowledge. Rather, some knowledge arrives directly, bypassing the normal cognitive filtration. However, in this mortal life, we are allowed to have our earthly personalities and intellects, our selves (with the small "s"), and to filter information through our past thoughts and experiences, thus changing it to suit our viewpoints. Even information received directly from the Divine Source is instantly transformed by us into something slightly different as it passes through our filters. But putting ourselves more directly in touch with the Source can increase the purity of the revelations. It may be sensed that the less we depend on our intellectual filters and the more we depend on unhindered spiritual inspirations, the closer we will be to the overall Truth of the Numinous.

This also means that no one person can receive inspiration for others because revelation is a personal affair. Leaders are very important in initial guidance, but often there are well-meaning leaders who try to dictate belief systems and dogmas to large groups of people and hold on to them permanently. Actually, they can do just so much in a general sense, and it is still up to the individual to receive what is right for him or her at the moment. No one else can know what we ourselves really and specifically need. So, to understand the things of the Spirit, we need to have information that comes more directly from spiritual sources, not through other people.

To aid in this quest, we need to open up to the "Self," which lets us glimpse truth that is not quite so subject to our supposedly rational thinking and interpretation as it is through the self. Often, inspiration just comes to us when we relax and open ourselves to it, most notably in meditation. Many scientific discoveries have been made through sudden flashes of inspiration or serendipitous juxtapositions. Yes, we understand that much preparation, education, and prior work had been done, and that the inspiration generally came through the lines of study previously established, plus the effect of intention to accomplish something of importance, but the inspiration was often unexpected, such as the discovery of penicillin or of X-rays.

As we saw before, it could be argued that dealing with individual Intuition could lead to chaos if each person marched to his or her own drummer. This viewpoint only shows how we are not yet well-versed in the art of pure Inspiration, because the true Numinous would be an overall knowledge that is Total and Complete, perfect in every sense, a unity of all thought in One. This is the state to which we can look forward when we all recognize ourselves as being one with Deity and, therefore, one with everything else without earthly fragmentations. This is a state that probably only exists when we are completely in tune with Spirituality without all of the impediments built into us during this mortal life. We cannot rationalize ourselves into this state, and it can only come when we allow spiritual inspiration rather than earthly hunches to flow.

As a side note, there are those who have had great success in receiving information from some unseen source by using such techniques as swaying or arm resistance to a pushing force. This indicates that the information is out there in a form we do not see. Others have past-life regressions, and can even share with others the elements of past lives that they had in common. Others might be seers, able to read other people, even in absentia, and foretell events. Others might deal in channeling, still others in the effects of crystals, still others with pendulums, and all generally able to tap into sources of information because it exists all around us. Actually, the Unity of all information explains many psychic phenomena, both because thoughts generate electromagnetic energy that can travel forever and so are always out there, and because everything exists in a constant Unity of Now.

In this book, we will refer to the spiritual side of intellect as Intuition or Inspiration, whichever word the reader chooses personally, and as we factor in this aspect, we will find ourselves opening more and more to heightened awareness, greater insights, more spiritual relationships, more highly-illuminated conclusions, and other phenomena of awareness that are not quite so tied to our rational processes or to the material world in general. We just let the information that is out there in the universe, the enlightenment and understanding from the Continuity of the Numinous, become apparent to us and enter our awareness directly.

Again, this is a personal thing, and the Intuitions of one person will not necessarily be those of another. If we were in a state of pure inspiration, washed by the Knowledge of Omniscience, all inspirations to all people would be the same, but in the here and now of our present material world, truth (as we will see in our look at the quantum) is not absolute, but rather is tailored to the individual who is seeing or measuring it. Therefore, everyone will get different Intuitions. This is fine for the moment. It is why this book gives only suggested Principles for the Numinous Factor, since each person can develop a different set according to personal needs and aspects of awareness. The Principles suggested here are just indicators that point one way for each person to see the concept of the Numinous and develop individualized interpretations; they are explained in detail just to start the process. What is important is to allow intuitive thoughts the chance to appear and to be recognized, an act that takes some effort in the beginning.

It is well to consider here the role of mysticism in all of this. Mysticism carries the idea of relating to Deity through direct personal experience, bypassing normal human perception and rationality. It really means the same as intuition. It is the recognition and practice of relating to the Numinous directly. It is not mysterious because that word comes from a different root. It can be a high-level and liberating concept for the person who deals in Intuition to think of himself or herself as a mystic, a person who receives inspiration from the Source rather than through intermediaries, able to rise unfettered to whatever level of spirituality may be right at this moment. Leaders, however, are often necessary to point the way and provide initial guidance, and certainly should be consulted. Group meetings can be very helpful also. But when a person is ready to act on Intuition and be a mystic, it will be apparent, and the ability to soar will be manifest.

Intuition, then, has to do with Spirituality, with a direct relationship to a Higher Power in an effort to understand aspects of the physical world. It deals with our own spiritual natures, our Selves, which are part of, and yet different from, our physical bodies. To see this a little better, we have to turn to the concept of Consciousness.

Consciousness

Consciousness refers to awareness, to our realization of the things around us and our place among them. It is an invisible essence, an energy field that gives light and awareness. Let us imagine ourselves sitting in a concert played by a symphony orchestra. The members of the audience might illustrate various aspects of consciousness. One person will be asleep, and so mostly unconscious. Another will be drowsy and so only semi conscious and just partly aware of what is going on. Another may be aware of the concert but hate the whole thing in a state of negative awareness. Another may have the ability to be aware also, but is dwelling so much on other thoughts that awareness only comes from time to time. Another will hear everything, but not be sufficiently prepared to know what the music is trying to do. Another will be very aware and will be rationally analyzing the music and what is agreeable or disagreeable about it according to his standards. And another will be hearing and understanding, and will be carried away by the beauty of it all, existing in a state of joy that could be considered akin to a sublime spiritual experience. It can be seen that, in order, these represent unconsciousness, semi-consciousness, destructive consciousness, distracted consciousness, limited consciousness, rational consciousness, and spiritual consciousness. They climb the ladder from the most rudimentary to the highest levels. For example, the rational person may be more aware of the beauty of the music than the limited person, but be too bound up in thought to let go and enjoy the sublime beauty felt by the person who is beyond thoughts.

Consciousness, then, is awareness, and is able to exist at various levels of intensity. Consciousness is the creating and experiencing element. Without it, nothing can exist for us. We are dead to it all. It is interesting to note that Oriental sages often speak of "chi," or "qi," the flowing life energy that keeps the body balanced. The body takes in chi from the outside and moves it about, keeping life flowing in us. This flowing energy cannot be seen through physical observation or measurement, but has to be inferred from its results, much as the wind itself is not seen but only its effects. Likewise, higher consciousness cannot be seen but its effects become readily apparent to the sensitive observer. This speaks for the existence of the Numinous as the Living Consciousness behind the Creation of everything in this Universe and in other universes that may exist. Thus, if our own weak consciousnesses are an element of this Supreme Essence, they can be raised to awareness of the Numinous and of the Peace and Oneness of all Creation in balance. Specific questions of physics really become moot when our enlightened awareness sees the infinity of Creation as one complete and perfect Now.

But consciousness seems also to be a combination of knowing and doing. Knowing without doing is like reading a book about how to ride a bicycle; the full benefit just is not there. To raise our limited earthly consciousnesses higher in awareness of the Numinous, we can continue to apply the elements of EMILY, which will open our eyes to what we need for rising still farther in consciousness, and all this can lead us to the Enlightenment that leaves behind our ignorance, fears, and self-centeredness, and instead immerses us in the happiness and peace of the Numinous.

How does all of this apply? The person who hates the whole subject of questions about the Universe will stay mired in behaviors that ignore the whole subject. The limited person will wonder, but not be able to realize many answers. The distracted person will glance at the subject from time to time but not stay long enough for an awareness to build. The rational person, often the scientist, will certainly find answers to many factual situations, but will possibly be so intent on what seem to be facts or on looking for factual errors that spiritual inspiration, the door to true knowledge, will be missed. Only the truly spiritual person will allow Intuition to bring information to the fore and allow this energy field of consciousness to bring answers that already exist out there in the eternal Now. Knowledge is all around and consciousness records it so that this information is available to those who allow the visions of it to overcome the angers or distractions or even humanly logical thoughts of the day. Therefore, regardless of how many rational things we may look at in this book, we will gain more understanding and awareness by allowing our higher spirituality to develop, especially when we use EMILY as our guide. The trick is that the limited person, the rejecting person, the distracted person, and even the wholly rational person do not have to exist. They represent earthly characteristics. By opening ourselves to the steps of EMILY leading to Enlightenment, all of us can be receptive to the fullness of the Numinous. Differences among us that the ego insists on seeing will just fade away and we will feel oneness with everyone and everything as we sense their spiritual essences. This state can be the state of Enlightenment in the spiritual definition of the word.

So Enlightenment is the practical means of achieving awareness and application of the principles of the Numinous Factor. The word usually refers to receiving instruction or knowledge, but the concept of "light" in its name is well beyond that. We will use it to refer to more than just gaining facts, but rather to having a spiritual light shine on previously dark things, making them luminous and clearly visible in their entire truth. Enlightenment is not just learning data, but is seeing the data clearly in their spiritual ramifications as well as worldly ones. It is similar to taking a crystal and looking at it in ordinary light to see the factual aspects of its shape, planes, structure, hardness, and the like, and then shining ultraviolet light on it to see its inner glow.

But the trick is that the ego-based self cannot be enlightened in this way. The ego holds a tenacious grip on our individuality and thinks itself to be our true identity. It seems that we cannot escape its pull since it has been doing this since our birth, so, as we will see later, only the spiritual Self can be enlightened. The ego, or self, with its need for dominance, for factual proof of everything, and for separateness from Deity, cannot.

Higher Vibrations

And here is the key point: Intuition deals with higher or richer consciousness, with higher or more complex vibrations, never lower ones. It is why spiritual people feel love, harmony, peace, and fulfillment when they are in touch with intuition. Lower vibrations seem to be more destructive in nature. This is not defining "good" or "bad," but showing the consequences of various beliefs, the karma. The result of being fully aware of the Numinous is great joy. It is why people have developed the idea of going to heaven when they die, not just through wishful thinking, but because the inspiration that does come through to them indicates a state of bliss when they are fully united with the Numinous, and their human thinking pictures material aspects of it, such as walking streets of gold, much as ancient people pictured Deity in terms of a tribal chieftain or petty king since that was the only kind of ruler they knew. We know much more now than they did, and we therefore have to move beyond these types of limited thinking, both in terms of Deity and in terms of revelations through that Deity.

To see how this can be done, let us use an acoustic guitar with nylon strings. The top and bottom strings are tuned to the same note two octaves apart, and the next lower string is tuned to a harmonic of them. If we pluck the top string, and then stop it from vibrating, we hear the note go on. We can do this over and over and always get the same result. It is not just a long echo from the resonance box, as some people think. If we do it again and touch the bottom string, or even the string next to the bottom one, we find that they are the ones doing the vibrating. We wonder how, since we did not touch them when plucking the top string. The answer is that the vibrating motion of the top string sets up waves that allow the other strings to vibrate in harmony with it. Opening our awareness even more, we realize that the strings tuned to the lower pitch have subdivided their lengths on their own so that they can vibrate at the higher pitch of the top string! Furthermore, we note that this only works when the lower strings are tuned either to the basic pitch of the top string, or to a harmonic of it. We realize a great concept: Spiritual inspiration can allow us to vibrate in harmony with it to create a beautiful sound, but only if we are in tune in the first place. This takes some effort on our part.

This is the function of Intuition, and we will see later how it is one of the attributes of the Numinous present in all of these Principles. The vibrations of the spiritual energy become our energy of vibration in harmony with it in happy, uplifting, and positive energies, which concept takes us to the last Principle, that of going from Elements to Energy.

Elements versus Energy

We are accustomed to referring to carbon and hydrogen as elements. And we are accustomed to referring to a chair or a table or a rock as a physical thing. We touch them, manipulate them, measure and dissect them, and just accept the concept that everything tangible has substance or matter. But science also tells us that a table is made up mostly of empty space. If we take a hydrogen atom, for instance, which has one proton and one electron, and enlarge the proton until it is the size of a small marble, its electron will be the size of a speck of dust, orbiting it 150 feet away. To picture this, if we were to suspend that marble from the 15th floor of a 30-story building, the electron would orbit from the ground to the roof 30 stories up. Obviously, everything in between them would be empty space. The marble, of course, would be so small as to be invisible at that height, and the electron completely invisible anyway.

But the situation will get even more interesting when we look at quantum mechanics and at what things make up protons (quarks) and what things make up the quarks, and we finally get to the bottom of it and find that there is really no matter at all involved in a chair or a rock or an atom or anything; they are all made up of vibrating energy. Everything is energy.

Energy is generally defined as the capacity for doing work. It does not necessarily refer to something tangible. It means a flow sufficient to move something, and as we see when watching light photons spin a paddle wheel inside the little jar, it does not take much power in the physical sense. Power in its physical definition just means the rate of doing work. If something moves very fast, there probably is a lot of power behind it. But even in our cells, low-power energy brings in fuel, burns it, moves out the waste, repels invaders, and duplicates the cell through growth. All this is movement and all is energy.

And we know that energy cannot be created or destroyed, only transformed. Look at what happens when we apply the brakes to our car. We have burned fuel to give the car energy to get up to speed, so the fuel consisting of stored energy was transformed into propulsive energy for the car. When we stop, we apply the brakes and the car slows down. To where does all that kinetic energy go? Much of it is dissipated as heat, as we will painfully find out if we touch the brake drum. And a tiny part of the brake drum itself disappears as well, also transformed to heat. If the input and output are measured, nothing is lost. To stretch things a bit, maybe that heat helped a plant to grow by the roadside, and it, in turn, got eaten by a passing horse which thus received the energy from the car brakes and used some of it to pull the car from a mud hole farther down the road, and on it goes. The energy of the Universe circulates around and around and none of it is lost.

It is very intriguing to contemplate what it is that keeps this energy circulating. Does it do it all by itself? Or could there be some Entity that supplies the intelligence and impulse for movement? If energy is the most basic thing in the Universe, what could be more basic or could exist separately from it to do this? Well, one might contemplate that only the Numinous could be that Entity. Through Omnipotence, the Numinous has all the power, meaning energy. Through Omniscience, the Numinous is the Intelligence in everything. And through Omnipresence, the Numinous exists everywhere in the Universe. So the Principle that everything is energy is as vital to an awareness of the Numinous as the other four Principles. The Numinous is the only Reality of the Universe because the Numinous constitutes everything in the Universe and everything is energy.

This concept may not be clear now, but will be of the greatest importance later in our study, especially when we realize that, if all the solid matter in the Universe could be compressed down so that no space existed within it (assuming that the immense repellent forces would allow that), estimates of the resultant size of this object range from the size of a thimble down to the size of a pea, and even that would be nothing but energy. So, the more we factor Energy into the seeming solidarity of mass, the more we will see the true nature of the Universe, which is energy.

This energy can take many forms of outward nature, but there can also be many internal aspects. For instance, gravitational attraction occurs when one mass pulls another mass toward it, such as how the earth pulls the moon and keeps it in orbit, but the moon also pulls the earth and this can be seen in the tides. The water does not fly off to the moon since the earth attracts it with more power, the same power that lets us walk about on the earth thinking that our heads are up. This is done by the various masses exchanging basic particles called "gravitons," the smallest units of gravity. The constant back-and-forth exchange between different quantities of gravitons alternates between potential (stored) energy and kinetic (moving) energy, and attraction results. But what is not widely known is that the graviton, which itself is just energy, is able to escape the confines of this Universe in a way that light cannot. It is done through a process that we will see later, and means that the graviton could be attracting energies, and even intelligence, from outside our known existence. It is intriguing to consider the possibility of shaping the frequencies of the graviton to carry information or intelligence back out again, much as an electromagnetic carrier wave can have radio programs fed onto it either by frequency modulation (FM) or amplitude modulation (AM) to be then broadcast to our receivers. Since this possibility is apparently not discussed much in scientific circles, it remains another of the elements of the Numinous to be sensed through Energy, Limitlessness, and Intuition.

CHAPTER FIVE

● ● ● ● ● ● ● ● ● ●

Seeing Spirituality in the Principles

The Principles

So here again are the five Principles of the Numinous Factor in table form. As you will remember, it is suggested that, for spiritual growth, the materialistic term on the left needs to be multiplied into our viewpoints to a lesser and lesser degree, while the term on the right needs to be multiplied into our viewpoints to a greater and greater degree.

> Limitation ⇨ Limitlessness
> Uniqueness ⇨ Unity
> Cause ⇨ Continuity
> Intellect ⇨ Intuition
> Elements ⇨Energy

We also remember that reading about these paths to higher consciousness is only part of what we will need to achieve this increase in spirituality. Like learning to ride a bicycle, we can accomplish just so much by studying, and then we must actually get on one and ride it, catching ourselves or even falling once in a while until we perfect ourselves in it. So, to understand the things of the Numinous, we really need to participate in them, to actually *be* them. We can do this by remembering the spiritual principles of EMILY that we should be practicing all along as we continue with our study:

Enlightenment
Meditation
Intention
LOVE
Yielding

So, how shall we use the Principles of LUCIE in the mode of EMILY to get a glimpse of the functioning of the Numinous Factor itself, to see better the truths of the Universe beyond what the physical senses can show, to see the spiritual side of Creativity?

The process is simple: We take each Principle to infinity. Let us see just how this can be done.

Infinity

Infinity is an area outside of human control and rational understanding. It is the realm of Deity, a realm not even comprehended by humans. How can we pretend to reduce Deity to our terms of understanding when we do not know the wholeness of just this Universe, much less of any other universes or of the Nature of Deity outside of the Creation? How can we have the audacity to proscribe the Fullness of the Divine when most of the matter of just this Universe is called dark matter because we do not understand much about it, and almost all of the energy is called dark energy because we do not understand it either? How can we pretend to eliminate Divinity from the scheme of things when we do not know where any of this came from or where it is going or what its cyclical nature might be? No, the Divine is infinite and It is in everything. Any attempt to limit or ignore any consideration of the Divine in our scientific or personal studies leaves us with an incomplete and flawed picture.

We, therefore, need to shed our limits and, instead, see the Principles of the Numinous in their infinite forms. We can start by taking Limitlessness to its infinite state, and then apply this method to the other Principles in like manner. For the Numinous to be accessed correctly, there must be total Limitlessness in our awareness and complete lack of restrictions on our thinking. We cannot limit the size and complexity of this Universe in our minds because we are aware of only a small part of it. Likewise, we cannot limit its number of dimensions, the number of possible parallel universes, the amounts of energy or manifestations in it, or its place in the overall scheme of things. After all, there might be so many universes that this one of ours might be whirling around the center of something far more immense, much as the way our sun, with its planets, is whirling around the center of the Milky Way Galaxy. We can examine this later. But maybe there are billions of universes like ours rotating around some vast center that we cannot even imagine with our earthly limitations. Therefore, we cannot assign restrictions to our view of the Deity that might actually be the substance of this awesome view. We must take off all restrictions to our thinking and engage in complete Limitlessness, using Intuition to allow us to sense something much greater than we have been able to imagine so far because of our earthly thinking.

We can see the other Principles in the same way. Unity taken to infinity, for example, means that everything that exists, whether here or in other realms, whether visible or not, whether manifested in the form of matter or still extant as invisible energy, whether existing now or in the "past" or yet to be formed, is united in Oneness as part of the Divine. This has to be an infinite unity, being beyond our scope of knowledge and almost beyond our ability to imagine.

Let us think about that a bit. We saw earlier the way that carbon came into being and then came here. It probably came from a star, where it was formed in the intense heat of the fusion process, and then was blasted into space when the star exploded. Apparently, there is a unity that bridges immense distances and time warps to unite your body with that of a star. And, of course, the carbon atoms are made up of nuclei and electrons, and all the building blocks or quarks that built the nuclei could have come from other atoms and could have formed still others, and so all the parts are in the unified whole and can be used again and again in any part of it. What is at the base of all this that gives form to all these parts? Is there anything completely firm and unchangeable?

A little reflection could indicate that yes, there is: the Numinous. Atoms can come together in almost an infinite number of ways to form entities, and then recombine to form others. The only unchanging thing is the unity that keeps everything tied together so that combinations can occur. The question could then arise about whether there is a Cause, a Deity that makes all of this happen, as so many believe? No, because that would indicate duality, the idea that Deity as a so-called First Cause is separate from the elements that are being used to create. Rather, if the Deity *is* the elements, then the combining is just part of the Continuity, and thus, the Unity.

Therefore, it can be seen again why we cannot assign "causes" to anything. We do not have enough knowledge to do so. We can just accept that everything is part of the great Continuity, the on-going nature of All that Is. Everything just arises from this great continuum as part of its nature, as part of the Divine. If we try to identify a cause to anything, we instantly limit it, and we do not know enough to do so.

Intuition helps the person who is in tune to bridge the gap in knowledge. Intuition comes from areas beyond our ability to understand. Knowledge exists everywhere, all around us, because of Omniscience and Omnipresence, but we cannot comprehend all of it. Only a little bit can get through, and even that has to be instigated for us because we do not know enough to instigate it for ourselves. Therefore true Intuition is ineffable, not like the simple ideas we create in our heads as part of our wishful thinking or like our claim to know what is best for us and for others. Intuition comes from a greater source than our limited thoughts. It is not logical according to our concepts of logic, and it is not necessarily specific due to its ethereal nature in consciousness levels that we have not yet attained. So we cannot assign any finite limitations to it and must accept it as infinite and as coming from the infinite Numinous.

And as for Energy, do we think we can assess the amount of energy there is in just this Universe? Until the atom bomb, we had no idea of the vast untapped energy in a simple rock out in the desert. Einstein defined energy as mass times a constant, the speed of light squared. But how much mass is really around us when we cannot see or measure most of the mass we think is in the Universe since we cannot see it? What about the energy in other universes, or even just galaxies, that we have not seen yet? How can we presume to limit it? We do not know the extent of Creation, we do not know anything about black energy, and certainly know nothing about energies beyond this Universe! We do not know the limits, so how can we think to place them? And since matter is energy, everything that exists is really energy and it is all part of the Divine Continuity of All That exists, and so is as fathomless as is the Nature of the Divine.

So taking each Principle to its infinity leads inexorably to the Divine unless, as some may argue, there is no Deity at all in this and that the Universe is an infinite succession of existences that just are and always have been, a variation of the monkeys with typewriters view. This is all well and good. As was pointed out in the Preface, this book is not meant to prove anything, but rather to indicate a spiritual path that the reader may want to try, a path that could lead to a heightened ability to receive intuition. After all, it might be easier to believe that a large, fully-equipped luxury automobile could spring completely assembled and running perfectly out of a mountain of iron ore than to believe that this Universe, with its fantastically complex organization and tremendous forces held in delicate balance, both in outer space and in the subatomic world, just came into being by itself. It also could be argued, however, that with enough universes, one such as this might eventually evolve in this form. If this is how readers wish to believe, that is fine, because that is their path at the moment. However, Intuition might supply a different outlook if it is applied properly, so it might be well for us to look into the Numinous Factor as pictured herein and see what insights might be forthcoming through Intuition. It could be worth the try.

Applications

Limitations are hard to overcome because we take them so much for granted that we do not necessarily realize that they are there. For instance, we have always believed that living beings, such as animals or humans, had to have a physical makeup that was based on carbon, oxygen, and potassium, among other elements. We can now read in the newspaper of experiments in which some bacteria that were fed a compound with the potassium removed and arsenic, normally a poison, added in, were able to thrive! Microbes live in radioactive rocks, in thermal hot springs, in volcanoes, in extreme acidity, in extreme alkalinity, and under extreme pressure. Knowing this means that our old ideas of what constitutes living beings have to be reassessed. We now have to admit that there may well be other life forms out in space that are based on other groupings of elements. Our limited thinking concerning living beings must now expand, and even our concept of "life" must change. We can take all this to infinity by sensing that an infinite number of different life forms can exist, many having no need for oxygen or carbon. We have no concept of how this can be done, right now, but we can at least see that our prior limited thinking now has to expand.

It is interesting to see that visible space as we know it is not empty, but is filled with movement and activity, of energy and matter, of behaviors that we are just learning to understand a little. But the fact that so much of the visible universe is organized and orderly leads us to the conclusion that there is not random chaos in the rest of the Universe, and we can sense the guidance of the Numinous.

We have to go to the principle of Limitlessness because we have no idea what the limits are in almost everything we can contemplate, let alone what we cannot yet even imagine. What is the limit of "hot?" what is the limit of "small?" What is the limit of "intelligence?" For us to leave behind our limits and go instead to complete Limitlessness, we have to feel confident that we will not be left hanging by fickle reverses of a chaotic state, and therefore we have to depend on the existence of the Numinous, which not only makes things happen, but also gives meaning and organization to it all. It is interesting to note that complete Limitlessness seems, in our human view, to lead toward chaos and complete breakdown. Actually, the Universe itself is well-organized, down to the smallest particles, and goes on operating year after year in about the same ways. This bespeaks an Organizer, able to make an organized state the greatest example of Limitlessness.

It is like a stand-off at a street intersection with no traffic control. Car A tries to enter the intersection and gets halfway across, but cannot proceed because car B has entered from his right and is blocking him. However, car B cannot move either, because car C has entered from his right and is blocking him. Of course, car C cannot move out of the way because car D has entered from his right and is blocking him. Car D cannot move because we already saw that car A has entered the intersection and is blocking him. Each car blocks another and no one can move, but there had been the absolute freedom of having no traffic control, meaning that any car was at liberty to enter the intersection whenever it wanted to. Leaving was just a different matter. Traffic chaos produced a gridlock and no movement. There is far more limitlessness in an orderly control of traffic flowing in and out of the intersection than in uncontrolled chaos. The key is in the intelligence involved, the enlightened viewpoint of each driver to see that insisting on having his own way without regard to the whole is destructive. Each could adjust his speed or could apply common sense and courtesy for the good of the whole to allow traffic to proceed freely through the intersection. This is higher knowledge than individual selfishness or lust for power or for control, some of the traits usually thought of as destructive and of lower vibrations.

So we should use unlimited thinking along with regard for the whole in seeing overall truth in order to understand the Universe. Total Limitlessness is actually putting ourselves into the overall Good of the Numinous, an act of higher consciousness than that of unfettered license, and does not lead to chaos because it is part of the nature of Unity.

Unity taken to infinity gives us a oneness that is beyond atoms, tables or stars. It takes the organization that we can see and elevates it to a complete and perfect Totality that includes all the forces and manifestations that we can see or measure as well as all the ones that we cannot. There can be no such thing as error in the infinite unity. Whatever exists must be correct in its own sphere. Something can be different in another sphere or dimension or parallel universe, but that does not destroy the nature of what is perceived here. Our very perception is part of the Continuity of the Universe, as we shall see in how wave forms in the quantum collapse into particle forms differently for different observers or measurers. Therefore, what we perceive and our perceptions themselves must be part of Unity when it is taken to infinity, regardless of our seeming differences of opinion. And if we are aware of the Numinous, then that awareness is part of the Unity also, and even if our perceptions are limited at the moment, the full nature of Numinous is the Unity, whether we can conceive of that totality now or not.

Continuity carried to infinity is where we really see the operation of a Supreme Being. Taking it to infinity means that everything that seems caused by something else now is actually a part of the overall Continuity, the spontaneous rising of everything out of the continuous Creation that seems to be part of the basic Nature of the Numinous. Carried to Infinity, Continuity is the totality of everything as part of the Eternal Now of the Numinous, and thus there is no succession of causes. Everything just is, in a complete and harmonious state of Oneness. As we saw before, Continuity can be even bigger than that: If our Universe consists of electrons revolving around atomic nuclei, of planets revolving around suns, of stars revolving around the centers of their galaxies, just what is to prevent this Universe from being an entity in another huge system, revolving around the center of it, and on and on through an infinity that is hard to even imagine?

Intuition seems, at first glance, to be unique among the Principles because, due to its nature, it needs to come from a Source. It is a knowledge that is imparted. It has structure and an antecedent that allowed it to manifest. It is organized and comprehensible. Taken to an infinite nature, it comes from the totality of the knowledge of the Universe, which is all One. By its nature, it implies an Agent that does the imparting and a purpose for the information. All this is a part of the Numinous.

And we have seen before how all is Energy, an energy that gets organized into manifestations whether seen or unseen, and does not just exist chaotically. The infinite nature of energy is the total energy of the Universe and beyond. It is formed by vibrations that are maintained over time to give consistency, and there is no limit to vibrations. As we know, energy cannot be created or destroyed, only changed in form. Since that is so, then the question naturally arises: From where did the energy come originally? It is easy to see the answer when we reflect on what energy is. It is the totality of the vibrations of the Universe, all of which is the Numinous. As the Numinous is infinite, energy is infinite. It existed before the stars and their galaxies did, and is the Sum of everything that is.

Therefore, when we take the Principles of the Numinous Factor to the level of infinity, we see how they describe the Presence of a Creative Power in everything. Some will see this as the Numinous actually present in everything throughout the Universe as part of the vital makeup of its manifestation. Others may see it as an influence of a Deity Who still maintains the form with which they identify. Others can see it as an individual spiritual essence of a different sort for each thing that it inhabits. Others will see it as a creative energy, but at such a high level that it has greater power than anything else. However it is seen, it is the Numinous, and seeing its Presence is an important step to understanding the makeup and functioning of the Universe, the quantum world, and the physical world around us.

CHAPTER SIX

. . . .

The Factor and the Quantum

Light

Now, let us use the Principles of the Numinous Factor to see spirituality in some interesting views of the Universe. We will start with the world of the atom. This will not be difficult reading, but will show the value of having spiritual insight to see how everything really works.

Physicists were puzzled for many years by light, which behaved sometimes as if its little photons (or most basic elements) were particles, and other times as if they were spread out as waves. Various experiments and theories were devised to see which of these forms was the correct one since, in our Newtonian concept of physics, things have to be either one or the other.

Just one well-known scientific experiment will illustrate this. When a light source is firing photons through a slit in a barrier placed between the light source and a receiving screen, the photons act like particles and go straight through the slit and hit in one place on the screen. They make a large light patch on the screen. Now, if a second slit is opened alongside the first, this creates the possibility of interference among the particles as they go through both slits, and so now the photons behave like waves, bending around the slits as they go through and leaving a tell-tale pattern of light and dark interference circles on the screen, the same pattern made by water waves and all other waves under similar circumstances.

What is more, these two phenomena occur even when the photons are fired so slowly through the slits that they do not actually collide or interfere with each other: With one slit open, there is one lit place on the screen, whereas with two slits open there is the light-dark wave pattern. One answer could be that they take these positions from sensing that collisions might occur, which means that they have awareness. Another is that they are choosing other paths rather than the most direct one and these paths result in possible collisions. Possibly their wave-particle form allows them to behave in both ways, changing from particle to wave as they travel. Either way, one has the eerie feeling that they are able to make decisions as they go, a trait that is very hard for thinking humans to apply to particles of light.

Much of the answer to this lies in the field called "quantum physics." Quantum theory itself is from the early twentieth century. It gets its name from the concept that energy is thought of as being released in little packets called quanta. Quantum physics deals with the subatomic world, as opposed to the Newtonian physics of our material world, and to the Einsteinian physics of galaxies and outer space. It is completely different from them both, and scientists, including Einstein, struggled for years to find a way to combine these three systems of physics (and others that we may not know about yet) into one complete Theory of Everything. Scientists think that they may now be close, which we will see later on in this book. (Is that a teaser for you to keep on reading?) Although our look will be very simple, quantum theory is actually a very hard aspect of physics for scientists to grasp because there are so many variables in it, and the mathematics of it, which we will not look at, can be quite difficult.

Possibility versus Fact

The basic problem is that the quantum is a world of possibilities, not of certainties. Even when precise measurements are made of particles or waves, they only take us to the area of probabilities. When many, many observations and measurements are made, fairly predictable outcomes can be envisioned, but are by no means certain. It is a little like shooting an arrow in an arc and predicting where it will land by using launching force, arrow shape, arrow weight, the effect of gravity and added forces such as wind. The Newtonian physicist can predict the flight of the arrow without actually shooting it, and actual field trials will confirm his prediction because he was using fixed, well-established, and exact rules. The quantum physicist cannot make any such prediction with certainty; he can only say that there is a probability that the arrow will go to a certain spot since each arrow could wind up going to a completely different location than the one predicted due to a random nature that we do not yet understand fully.

What is even more unusual in the quantum world is that some arrows will affect others simultaneously with no visible means of interaction between them. What happens with this arrow over here is instantly reflected in that arrow over there, too fast for it to be done by any physical means that we know of. What is even worse is that firing the arrows at night when they cannot be seen will easily give a different result from doing it in the daylight because quantum theory indicates that just the act of being observed or measured will affect outcomes! All this will be seen in detail later, but it introduces us to a world of physical phenomena completely different from the one to which we have become accustomed. Later we will see how the Numinous makes all this much more comprehensible.

To return to our subject of light, quantum theory has indicated that, at the subatomic level, light and other phenomena can be described as *both* particles *and* waves. In fact, they can be the two simultaneously, but not to the same observer at the same time. A quantum phenomenon can have a wave form of possibilities, and then can collapse into one of many possible particle forms of actuality. As we saw with the arrows, the exact form it chooses cannot be determined with certainty and might even depend on the actual observation made of it! With different observers, different results can be obtained. Now, the two things needed to be known about a particle are its position and its velocity, the latter word being a term that includes the direction of travel. The way the quantum is, scientists cannot know both at the same time. The more they know about the one, the less they will know about the other. This is in no way the fault of the scientists. It is just the way the quantum world is set up. So the collapse of a wave form of possibilities into a particle of actuality is only predictable up to a level of probability, not of certainty.

Calculating Waves and Particles

Therefore, calculating waves and particles in the quantum world is very difficult. A particle is different from a wave in that it occupies a place and its location is known, but its direction and speed are not, as opposed to a wave which has no specific location and contains all the possibilities of the particles, but with a speed that can be calculated to an extent. This is why quantum equations are only equations of possibilities, not leading to specific fact or exact outcome as we are used to in the Newtonian world. They often are only forty percent accurate. This is very puzzling to scientists accustomed to precise outcomes, but using such equations to make approximations does give verifiable results, so they are valuable. It just makes the quantum world a strange one indeed!

Now, in considering how changes from wave form to particle form in the quantum seem to depend in part on observation or measurement, we see that the various wavelengths of light used to observe them add to the uncertain results and even affect the experiment overall. Short wavelengths show where the electrons are located, but also affect them so that we cannot predict their direction. Longer wavelengths let us see their trajectories and have less effect on them, but blur our view of the particles themselves. So just the act of measuring seems to affect such changes, or collapses as they are called. This is a difficult concept for the Newtonian world of "facts" to accept. The wave forms of possibilities collapse differently for different observers of the same waves using different measuring methods. In our Newtonian world, we expect one result for any action, and therefore the same result for all observers. Having every observer come with a different result may seem like chaos. We can wonder why there is not one exact truth that just occurs rather than many variations of truth through all the different observers, although we can get a hint of the answer by comparing various eyewitness accounts of the same crime scenario. They will often differ greatly due to the locations, abilities to observe, attentiveness, and personal biases of the observers. Thus it is sometimes difficult to say with certainty what the criminal action was.

Jumping

Here is another aspect of the quantum to put into the mix: Scientists have realized that electrons rotating around nuclei sometimes jump to another orbit for no apparent reason. This is often done with a resultant release of energy that can be seen as light, which is important since atoms themselves are not generally observable but the light they generate is, and this helps us understand electron jumping. There is an uncertainty element here that is puzzling. The jumps cannot be calculated in advance. Even after many observations and measurements, there is a low probability of predicting them, which is the way we have seen the quantum world to be. But what makes this even more interesting is that, before jumping, they seem to fuzzy themselves out over several orbits all at the same time as though checking the various paths they may take! They do this in their wave forms of possibilities and the actual jumping is a particle collapse.

This is a fascinating concept. It indicates that the various forms of the atoms can have several existences at the same time. They are not locked into being only "this" or "that" or "the other one," but can be all of them simultaneously. This indicates oneness, a unity that, in turn, indicates that there is no duality, as we pointed out earlier. With enough of an overview of the Universe, as from the viewpoint of Deity, everything can exist all at once and there is complete Unity.

Let us consider that carefully. We are used to thinking of time in a linear way, with everything happening in succession along a timeline that does not stop or reverse. We seem to see that one thing happens after another, and this helps give rise to the concept that one thing thus causes another. Yet, in the quantum world, electrons in their wave form can adopt various orbits *all at the same time!* Time itself does not pass until the electron actually settles or collapses into one orbit in a particle form, and that form can be different for different observers, and so the "time" involved can also be quite different and may even disappear. This gets very subjective, as opposed to the objective result we are accustomed to in the Newtonian world. A wave form is full of different possibilities existing all at the same time and all are real. This is a little akin to our thinking about what to do next in our lives and trying out several possibilities in our minds before actually deciding on one and physically doing it. Since everything that is "real" to us is experienced by the brain and consciousness, each possibility just as real as any other because we briefly live it in our personal awareness. What we can imagine is as real as what we see happen in front of us, and it can stir us to just as great an emotional response because the subconscious sees it as bona fide. For some people, playing beautiful music in their heads or remembering special past experiences can bring them to tears. So the electron has several "real" existences going on all at once. From the Relativity theories, we remember that two points connected by something less than the speed of light seem separated and seem to exist in a linear way. But as the speed of light is approached, time goes slower and slower, until at the speed of light time no longer passes and everything is in an eternal Present and is one. Is this not the fulfillment of the Numinous?

Speaking of which, it seems that this might be a good time to pause, take a breath, and reflect on other ways the Numinous gives us some insight into these phenomena.

Amplifying the View

Let us back up a little and apply the Factor. The Numinous Itself reminds us that our function in this book is to see the spiritual component to situations, and to realize that ultimately everything is spiritual, but we should work up to that concept slowly. We remember that it helps to put ourselves into a mode of actually trying to see spirituality instead of trying to fault the search. If we set our intention to see spirituality, we will enter that mode and we will have a greater propensity to see it. It is a little like buying a new red car: We suddenly tend to notice and identify a little more with the other red cars that we see. We are in a red car mode. If we do not now enter into the spiritual mode, we will be dependent on these words here as proofs, and they are not that because spirituality cannot be proven. When we took the Principles to infinity in the last section, we set up a propensity to see their spiritual side, and that would stand us in good stead here.

It would be a little like trying to prove the beauty of a piece of music: One can analyze it and look at the mathematical relationships between the levels of vibration (the notes), the intricate play of the harmonies and sub-harmonies, the varying rates of change of these vibrations (the tempo), and all the rest, but they will still not prove the beauty of the piece. Not only do some pieces gain their beauty by breaking strict rules of balance and the like, but even appreciation of the proper arrangement of all the elements still depends on an aesthetic sense that is the basis of the original question anyway. Each of us has a background and a level of appreciation that affects our liking or disliking certain things. It is subjective, not objective. The saying is that we can build machines to play notes, but it takes humans to create music. So, to appreciate beauty, we have to be in the aesthetic *mode*. Likewise, to see spirituality, we have to be in its mode, and that act takes intention on our part. Let us use that concept as we look at the Factor.

A quantum world with the complexity of ours does not function with the precision it presently has if sixty percent of its functioning is unknown guesswork. Unless all this fantastic complexity is just random chance, it seems that a Power would need to exist that understands and controls all of it. Perhaps factoring in the Numinous will give a little more insight and show us that there is most assuredly an Intelligence behind the whole operation, whether we comprehend it or not. As we have seen, this Universe has been going on for many billions of years without us and our reasoning abilities, so we might need to be careful about assuming that we can or do understand all that composes it.

The same will apply to the vastness of outer space as well as in the tiny subatomic world. Everything can be seen as pointing to the Numinous as being the Designer as well as being the Substance of it. Again, a Universe existing with the complexity of this one shows that it is not for lack of measuring abilities that man does not know all of the details; it is just inherent in the nature of the beast. Obviously, again, only the Numinous knows the true specifics. And we should note that Unity asks us to see everything as One, so there is no scattering or hodge-podge of particles and waves, but only one unified whole, functioning as one with the Numinous, the author of all of it, and all of us being a part of it with some sort of purpose.

Using the Principles

Let us consider the role of Limitlessness. Apparently, the quantum world of subatomic particles is freed from many of the limitations of the Newtonian world. Different results can be had from the same beginnings, particles can move for no reason that can be discerned, results of an action can be different for different observers, and everything seems to be interconnected to allow this over here to affect that over there in a seeming state of oneness. These results can be such a shock to us that we might have trouble believing them or changing our thinking to account for them because of our previous limitations. But we must do it because this quantum world does exist. After all, it took a major effort for peoples of the ancient world to accept the fact that the earth is not flat. To be able to understand more of this new world, we also have to shed our limitations in thinking of physics as only materialistic. The key in our thinking must be Limitlessness, the dropping of the limitations to our thinking. We can expand from, and are not bound by, old rules. We can see also that fluidity in the physical world indicates a need for us to be flexible in our thinking. We remember the Biblical story of putting new wine, which will ferment and expand, into old wineskins, which have already stretched and lost their elasticity. The old, inflexible wineskins can rupture with the expansion of what is put into them, whereas new skins can stretch. In like manner, we need to put all this new information and awareness into flexible minds that can expand to contain it all and not rupture.

Unity says that everything is One in the Numinous. Particles moving around in their own ways, protons changing their natures, outcomes varying according to the observers themselves, and other phenomena that we have seen all seem to be separate, yet must be one in some way in a togetherness that encompasses everything. Through Unity, we see that we humans and everything in the physical world are tied together by being one in the fabric of the Numinous. This concept can answer a lot of puzzling questions. One example will suffice: It has been observed that a spinning quantum particle here can affect the spin of another particle over there, and can do it instantaneously, therefore seeming to send its influence across the intervening space at a speed greater than the speed of light, which is impossible according to well-established proofs of Einstein's theories. But the explanation is simple if we see that the two particles are in unity with each other. The spin of one affects the spin of another because they are really of one body, as it were. This is why one arrow can affect another in our earlier example. They are united in a way that we cannot see, and yet it exists. Likewise, by seeing ourselves in unity with all around us, we can move with everything, understand more of it, and identify ourselves with it, making all the wondrous aspects of the physical realm ours in a way we cannot do when sitting on the outside trying to use pure logic from our very incomplete thinking processes. Chi Kung practitioners talk about sending healing energy over great distances. This can be understood when we realize that there is really no separation between the sender and the receiver since the flowing energy they use and call chi is really the fundamental matter of which the Universe is made, its oneness, its spirit, and it fills every bit of the expanse of the Universe as though everything were tied closely to everything else.

Intuition is the key to our understanding of all this. The mind that is closed to all but its own logical reasoning blocks itself from receiving the gentle intimations of Intuition from a greater Source. The more we factor in the Numinous, the more we are able to realize that there really is information held by a Higher Power, and the more we open ourselves to receiving it, the more complete will be our knowledge and reasoning abilities. As we noted earlier, some people use the resistance, or the lack of it, in pressing down the arm of another person while asking factual questions, reasoning that there is information "out there" that affects the flow of energy in the body, making the resistance of the arm either strong or weak if the answer is either positive/constructive or negative/destructive. Other people use swaying, or pulling apart locked fingers to tap into information, reasoning that thoughts are things and can be accessed. Others open themselves during meditation and allow Intuition to come. Others just relax, and the basic information already in the mind or the spiritual Self flows more freely.

For example, if we are stuck on a math problem or in solving a cryptogram, we can sit back and rest the brain a little, letting our mind wander idly. Often, solutions suddenly occur to us in this state. Or when we return to the work, we see with new perspective and then the problem is solved quickly. In the same way, when we relax in meditation, flashes of inspiration come to us. Some scientists and inventors admit that some of their most brilliant inspirations came in just this manner. When we learn how to carry a meditative sense with us while we are busy with other things, our minds can remain open to new perspectives, and solutions to other situations will occur to us. Is that from inspiration or just opening ourselves to sense new relationships and solutions? The answer is yes. Inspiration often comes from what is in us already because the Self is the part of us that deals in spirituality and it is always with us. When we listen to it, we think that we are receiving revelations, but the Self is in contact with all the knowledge all the time like a radio is always receiving signals but we have to turn it on and tune it in to hear them. Information is "out there" since the Numinous is Omniscient, and the Self is in open contact with the Numinous even when our egos temporarily block Intuition. Now, of course, getting answers through Intuition will often give different results to different people, as we commented on earlier, but we have seen that different observers receive different outcomes in the quantum world anyway, so this is to be expected, although it is certainly different from what we think we experience in the Newtonian world.

Continuity really helps in our view of the new quantum world. If we stick to the idea that everything is caused by something, we cannot understand why particles spring into being randomly, or how the many possible solutions to a problem can all be correct. The problem lies in our thinking that everything has to have a cause. In the first place, we have seen that human beings do not see facts, but only form opinions based on limited viewpoints. Everything we know is opinion. Scientists will be quick to admit that what they think to be true today may be found not to be true tomorrow. If they were to stick doggedly to their same, outdated opinions thinking them to be fact, they would still be thinking that the earth is flat and that the stars circle around us. But when we see all things as part of the Continuity of the Numinous, constantly ongoing and changing, constantly happening as part of the whole, constantly existing as individual parts of the Whole rather than being caused by some other entity, then we roll with it and allow everything to exist unfettered. We do not limit it with our restricted views of "cause." In the second place, things happen because they are part of the Unity of the Numinous. This is just a part of the nature of an Entity that is beyond our limited powers to understand. We not only accept and appreciate the power of a Mind much higher than ours, but, using Unity, feel that we and everything around us are a part of the Numinous and we can enjoy this unity with the peace of mind that comes from knowing that all is under control and is going well. In addition, further enlightenments occur to us when we do not insist on our own rigid structure of Cause.

Energy reminds us that we are not dealing with particles or things or individual mental interpretations, but only with energy. Materialistic things are just energy, thoughts are energy, and spiritual awareness is energy. These energies are interacting extensively, but they are still just energy, made of vibrations. Now, let us just consider something for a moment: If there is no real matter as a separate entity in the Universe, then from where did all of this energy come in the first place? What is the Power beyond it that keeps it all vibrating in just the right ways to maintain all that exists? If energy is the most elemental thing, beyond which nothing exists, then what is the Power that keeps it going? When we look at energy that way, the case for a sense of the Numinous becomes very strong. We can well realize that there is only one source that can keep all the vibrations of the most basic phenomena in the Universe in the correct order and all the frequencies extant in entities that do not exist except as energy, and therefore cannot control their own vibrations. Only the Numinous is the overall Designer and Coordinator, and keeps things growing and changing in order.

So particles, such as photons, are energy. They exist in one form, and can suddenly change to another form. They can get together to become part of an electron that is orbiting at the energy level one shell of an atom and suddenly changes to another level of energy in another shell. This is easy because they are all energy to begin with, and changing form or direction is simple, as we saw in the example of the brakes on our cars. Photons can exist as waves or as particles by being energy and can exist in several places at once by being potential energy that can go in any number of directions when it becomes kinetic energy. These things can seem puzzling to someone using nothing but human logic, but become quite clear when the spiritual component is seen.

Here is the key point: All this happens in the Numinous through the constancy of Continuity in which everything is Energy and, therefore, is all one in Unity, changing aspects as part of the Whole, all of which can be seen when we adopt Limitlessness as our viewpoint and expand to allow

Intuition to open our awareness. It should be pointed out that each reader is also part of the whole and will change aspect according to some of the criteria involved in his or her personal waves of creative energy. Again, the knowledge of this does not necessarily come as a scientific proof, but rather as an Inspiration, an insight that comes to us when we liberate ourselves from narrow thinking and instead focus on our spirituality, our personal Oneness with the Numinous. Is this provable to other people? Probably it is not. Even if they do open themselves to Intuition in a similar manner, their waves of potentiality will collapse into different particle forms as part of the creative process and their places in it. Probably every person reading this book will use different criteria to evaluate it, will receive different sets of interpretations and insights from it, and will act on these in ways different from the ways of other readers of the same materials. That is just fine. Whatever they receive is their reality at this moment and has a purpose. Those who reject everything here are also functioning as part of the infinite variety of Continuity, and that is just fine also.

CHAPTER SEVEN

● ● ● ● ● ● ● ● ● ●

Photons and Fields

Completing Equations

Now, let us go farther into the elements of the quantum world, and start by going back to the wave/particle situation that we saw earlier. The wave form of a piece of quantum stuff gives only a vague idea of its location since it can be spread out all over the place. But it does give a good idea of its momentum. Likewise, concentration on the position of the particle form of something gives a good idea of its location but only gives a fuzzy guess of its travel, whereas concentration on its velocity gives only a vague idea of its location. Again, none of this is through lack of skill of the physicists in measuring, but is inherent in the make-up of the quantum world. Since we have seen that location and velocity are the two ways of specifying quantum phenomena, it is obvious that we can only know possibilities, not actual facts, about the particles and waves. You just cannot get any more exact than that. However, when enough possibilities pile up, their overall numbers suggest a very good indication of probabilities, and therefore the equations work surprisingly well and are accurate in their predictions and verifications.

Well, if *we* do not know how to make the equations complete, who does? The Factor suggests that the Numinous does. There is no specific scientific evidence for this, nor is there meant to be, since it is our own decision as to how much of each Principle of the Factor we adopt. But the world of quantum physics shows us to a greater extent than do the other systems of physics just how dependent we are on having the Numinous being the essence of things. The subatomic world is so intricate, with such great forces held in exact balances, with huge masses of phenomena existing through vast stretches of space, with constant continuity and annihilation of particles, and with wave forms in all their complexities collapsing into different particle forms, that a person's spiritual sense suggests the existence of a Power controlling this whole process one-hundred percent and is not blocked by unknowns.

Of course, we could always say, as we did earlier, that our Universe is just one of countless universes that are trying to do the same things by random chance, and we are the ones who are succeeding, and that is why we do not see life forms in other systems, and if this is the argument that a reader wants to make, well and good, but there is a fallacy in this view. If everything is just random, what is to prevent a tree from suddenly flying off into its various components, or everything else in the world or the Universe just randomly changing into other forms, and even doing it over and over at great speed? If things just randomly fly together into a form, they can just as quickly fly apart again into other forms. What keeps a tree being a tree? What keeps a rock being a rock over billions of years? This concept suggests that there is order in the Universe, and not random chaos. It is far easier for us to see the organizing aspect of the Numinous in everything than to see random chaos, especially since the building of this type of view leads us to greater awareness in spiritual matters and a greater sense of peace and happiness in knowing that the Numinous is in control and that there is a purpose to everything.

Let us look at another fascinating concept in the wave/particle behavior, and to do so, we will return to the light-and-slit experiment. Scientists have seen that, with one slit open, photons go to a spot to which they would not go with two slits open, as evidenced by the dark area in the wave pattern on the screen at that point, as opposed to the light areas left by the direct beam. Could it be that the photons know ahead of time how many slits are open? They almost seem to have a consciousness of their own, something very difficult to believe in this Newtonian world where only living, thinking beings have consciousness. Or are there consciousnesses all around us in the trees, plants, even rocks and even the earth, which itself has been described often as a living entity? Well, that is what the Numinous is: the Essence that is in, as, and through all things, and is Life. There are various books about the living, feeling, reactive world of plants; there might even be such a book about rocks. If not, there should be.

Much of this concept is in LUCIE as a whole, because the Numinous indicates a presence of the Divine in everything, and therefore there is life in everything due to the living Nature of the Numinous. Everything, both seen and unseen, is energy, as we saw in Energy. There is unity in everything, as we see in Unity. Just as carbon atoms can be in animals and plants as well as in rocks, there is a relationship among all of them as part of the living, pulsating, energetic Universe, and Intuition can show us this beyond a rational view.

Using Limitlessness and Unity, we can expand our awareness of the Numinous enough to see a spiritual character both to photons and to the earth that is beyond our limited physical senses to detect. When we see everything around us as pulsating with the Numinous, the Spiritual nature of all that is; when we open our consciousness to higher ways of seeing the Continuity; when we really open our eyes to observe, rather than merely see, a physicality in everything, then the Numinous becomes more apparent. For now, we can just accept the thought and start to feel a closer affinity with the Universe around us, sensing that we are one with it, as Unity indicates.

Wave Collapse

Actually, we are more than that. As we saw before, many experiments in the quantum world have shown that, at the moment of observation or measurement of a wave of possibilities, the wave will manifest in a particle form that can be different for each observer or measurer. When we follow Continuity and Limitlessness, leaving behind our limitations and expanding our viewpoints with Energy as a base, we look at this scientific finding again and see that there is a creative element in the observation itself. Rather than just being passive observers, we become co-creators in the collapsing of the particle form. Note that we do not actually cause it to happen: Continuity reminds us that nothing causes anything, and that all just arises from the operations of the Numinous. There is, however, a power of Intention that allows an event to seem different for different observers, and this arises from the infinite realm of possibilities of wave collapse. Our intentions can set the scene for a specific collapse to happen. This is a propensity, not a cause.

How does this happen? We turn to Intuition to find out. Rather than try to discover an outward factual answer, we can turn inward and let our inner Self, the part of us that embraces spirituality rather than the worldly things of the self or ego, manifest answers in us through Inspiration. When we open ourselves to expansion and spirituality, and sense the Unity of ourselves with everything as part of the Numinous, we set the intention for information from the cosmos to come to us. Our part in Continuity is a little like listening to a work played by a large symphony orchestra. We can listen to the overall effect, or we can pick out our favorite instrument, say, a clarinet, and follow its musical line. When we focus on it, the sound comes to us because it was there all along as part of the whole. We are not creating anything as we listen to just that one instrument, but rather are allowing that particular particle aspect to manifest to us out of the wave of all the possibilities in the orchestra. Someone else could follow another instrument and have the sound of the orchestra manifest itself to them around that other instrument. In the world, then, when things exist in their wave form, all the possibilities are there and we just allow a particular one to take particle form in our consciousness through our power of intention. It was there all along as part of Continuity.

This is a spiritual element actually, because of the Continuity in us. As we join in the creative process, we emulate the Numinous in our own tiny, individual ways. As our consciousnesses grow to be able to realize this, they take greater roles in the Universe of possibilities, and we expand into other manifestations. All this is a part of the Continuity and Omniscience of the Numinous, and therefore the impact of our observation implies our own role in continuity and knowledge since the Numinous is all Continuity and all Knowledge.

Spiritual and Temporal Creation

Another realization from the Numinous inherent in all this is that all things are created spiritually as well as temporally. Since the Numinous is Omnipresent, there is just no such thing as a mechanical universe, set in motion by an Entity who then abandons it to run by itself. Let us make a simple analogy here. Just as how each of our actions in life is preceded by a thought, either at the moment or some time before, we can say for illustration that everything that is created by the Numinous has a spiritual thought or continuity as part of its physical manifestation. Of course, this is all simultaneous, since the Numinous is all there is, and is omniscient as well as omnipresent and omnipotent. There may seem to be sequence in the idea of "thought first, creation later," but all of it is Continuity. All of it is part of the ongoing Numinous. But it does indicate that we are allowed a part in the spiritual continuity by being a part of the Numinous. Our real advancement in this life comes from our *realizing* this and growing spiritually to match it, therefore achieving the Numinous in our consciousness.

It then follows that the spiritual and physical (temporal) are One. This means that anything we think, say, or do has a spiritual nature. We cannot compartmentalize or divide things into spiritual versus non-spiritual since all is Numinous, being in, as, and through all things, both seen and unseen, and so, even when we have thoughts that we may feel are unworthy of the Numinous, they are still part of our spirituality. What if the things that people think of and do are cruel and even vicious? We have to remember that good and bad are interpretations, judgments that often come from our limited perspectives and knowledge. The child can feel that it is cruel of his parents to take him to see the dentist, but the parent knows that this temporary discomfort is necessary in the long run. We saw earlier that, as we look at the Universe, we see seeming cruelty all over, from one animal on earth killing and devouring another to one galaxy sideswiping another in outer space, ripping off its stars and dust clouds unto itself. We may have trouble knowing which to regard as good, and which to regard as bad until we remember that these terms depend on human judgment, which is very fallible. Let us just use the Numinous, and accept with our spiritual natures that these things just are, and that everything is spiritual because the Numinous is in, as, and through all things, due to Omnipresence, Omnipotence, and Omniscience, and the Numinous does not deal in anything other than spirituality.

This can be even harder to see in such secular things as electrons, but spirituality is there too. Let us consider again the electron that jumps shells for no apparent reason or the particle that comes into being and then just fades back into the soup of the electromagnetic belt that exists everywhere. All this happens as part of Continuity and therefore is a part of the Numinous and therefore is spiritual. Those who must always see a cause for everything might consider Continuity and the idea that nothing causes anything, but rather, that everything comes about as part of the Continuity of the Numinous.

The Electromagnetic Field

Let us look at that electromagnetic belt for a minute. Scientists have made great progress in understanding the forces around us, and one of their discoveries is a big one. It has long been postulated that the supposedly empty spaces between atoms, between particles of atoms, between planets and the sun, and everywhere else in the Universe, are really filled with energy, and now it has been realized that there is an immense electromagnetic energy field that exists everywhere throughout the Universe. It is pulsating with energy, electrical charges, and jiggling particles springing into life and then being re-absorbed, as well as other phenomena. This field goes by many names, among which is Zero Point Field because it is considered to be active even at a temperature of absolute zero, a point at which all motion had been thought to cease. It is also known as the Electromagnetic Field. Through this Field, every particle in the Universe is constantly in motion, coming into being, exchanging energy, changing form, moving around at a dizzying rate, and then sinking again into the Field. Waves, too, are active and interactive, setting up vast amounts of possibilities, constantly setting the scene for manifesting particle forms, and reinforcing or dampening each other depending on whether or not they coincide. Continuity and change are constant.

In the Electromagnetic or Zero-Point Field, electric charges accelerating throughout space are coupled with magnetic fields doing the same. They affect each other, of course, as can be seen by how electric current is generated by rotating a coil of wire in a magnetic field. These fields race through space at the speed of light, a radiation that has effects everywhere. Protons have a plus electrical charge, and electrons have a negative charge.

These make up the atoms that are the building blocks of all matter, so the complex interactions of electricity and magnetism affect everything that is. The electromagnetic force is one of the four forces operating among elementary particles. The others are: the strong force, the weak force, and gravity. The first has to do with holding atoms together, the second with allowing decay, and the third is the familiar attractive force that we all know to some extent. These forces are kept in delicate balance, so that any variation of them could have cataclysmic consequences. It is hard not to feel that there is a Designing and Controlling Power behind them all.

The Electromagnetic Field, then, is filled with particles being created, decaying, and affecting each other over varying distances. It affects just about everything that we can see or sense, and might have even greater effects on the black energy and black matter that we have more difficulty seeing or sensing. This Field, of course, is part of the creative medium of the Numinous. It is a vast store of energy forms that arise, interact, and subside again, but since they are all Numinous, they are all one, and so are linked even in their diversities. Here is where Unity really comes into play. Through it, we can see that there is not one particle "here" interacting with one "there" because there is no here or there in the Oneness of the Numinous. As we saw earlier, that idea would be called "duality." In fact, everything is one in Omnipresence and in Unity, and there is no duality, no separation.

It has been noted, in addition, that one particle might have a particular spin and another particle might spin to match it, but this would be done so rapidly that the relationship would have to exceed the speed of light to actually go from one to the other, and this is impossible. Here, again, Unity shows us the answer to that great dilemma: Since all is One, there is a linking or unity between the two particles because they are one in the Numinous. They move together by virtue of being of the same Body. They do not cause each other to react, but they both rise in a linked form as part of Continuity. We humans are linked in the same ways, again according to Unity, but our egos prevent us from seeing what our spiritual natures would know instinctively were we fully aware. Since the Numinous is totally present all the time, and all energy is one Energy, then all knowledge and relationships are totally and continually present, and we can develop ourselves to be open and receptive to them. And, since all possibilities of continuity already exist in wave forms, our part consists in becoming aware of a particular form in our specific existence at this specific time and letting it collapse for us.

Some people might speak of the Numinous as being the First Cause, but it might be better to think of It as the Constant, or the Only Is. The Numinous is all that exists, and everything just exists as part of It. What seems to be creativity on our part is just awareness of a specific outcome among many possibilities. We recall from the Old Testament the importance of the time when Moses learned that the name of the Deity for him at that time was: "I AM." Since Hebrew, like Russian and other languages, rarely uses the present tense of the verb "to be," the use of it places great emphasis on it. The Numinous is the "I AM," the Self-Existent One, being All that Is whether recognized or not. Realizing this concept clarifies the Numinous, and it all comes through Intuition.

CHAPTER EIGHT

Other Universes

Infinite Universes

Let us look once more at waves, and specifically at the fact that an electron, in deciding to jump to another orbit or shell, does not just do it immediately, but behaves like a wave first, smearing itself out over the various shells as if trying each one on for size, but *all at the same time.* We note that it then makes the jump in a particle form. So wave forms contain all the possibilities and the particle form is the specific event at a specific time in a specific place. Actually, one of the possible reasons for light waves to run interference rings in going through the slits that we saw earlier, even when fired one at a time, is that each might take one of all the possible paths to the target, including detours and side trips, and can come in at any angle. The wave of possibilities is a quantum effect, but since all matter in the universe, regardless of size, is still made up of atoms and the subatomic quantum phenomena that include waves and particles, the wave is a vital element of all existence and of understanding the Principle of Continuity.

Here is one manifestation of that thought; if the electron can choose all of the various possibilities of shells to which it can jump and then picks one, do all the other possibilities cease to exist? Scientists are now considering carefully the concept of multiple universes based on this type of manifestation. If the electron picks just one possibility and jumps that way, there will be a domino effect of other happenings based on that jump, and therefore the universe unfolds from that point on in a particular way. If the electron had chosen another way to jump, the universe would have unfolded from that point in a different way. In fact, some feel that it is becoming evident that there are multiple universes: In one, the electron jumps this way, and in another, it jumps that way, and in a third, it does not jump at all. Each of these universes is valid, but each will unfold differently because of how the waves of possibility actually collapse. This allows each entity to achieve its complete fulfillment, and not be limited or stopped by the actions of another entity. If a person never learned to play the piano because there was not one in the house in youthful days, it is unfortunate that someone else's decision not to buy one has blocked the pleasure of fulfillment. For true limitlessness, there needs to be another universe wherein the piano is indeed bought.

Unity indicates that there can be an infinite number of universes, each developing along a line started by one particle jumping in a certain way, with the resultant domino effect. As can be seen, the number of universes must indeed be close to infinite, since there are so many pathways and networks that can result based just on the jump of one electron in one atom among all the possibilities available to it and with all the atoms in the whole Universe. But since the electron in this one lived out all of those possibilities already while still in its wave form, they should all tend to manifest. Since they cannot all do so in one universe, there may be multiple universes for this to come about, and this is another aspect of the Numinous.

Humans function the same way. If we have a choice to make among many options, we think about them carefully and so they all exist at once in our minds in a type of wave form. We try out each mentally and see where it might take us if we decide that way, much as good chess players analyze the various possible outcomes several moves ahead of the move they are contemplating. But when we make our choice, and the wave form collapses into that particular particle form, starting a domino effect of other choices in our life and in the lives of others affected by us, all of the other possible choices are still alive and each takes place in a subsequent domino effect, each of which creates another series of events.

When we choose one path, do all the rest cease to exist? Do we lock out succeeding events in the lives of other people by our choices and keep them from achieving some of their fulfillment by our actions? Is this fair to them? The infinite nature of the Numinous precludes that and so, by its very nature, the Numinous embodies infinite universes with every possible pathway coming to fruition. Anything less, and the Universe would cease to be infinite and the Numinous would not be complete.

When this is carried further, we human beings are living in one universe that has come about as a result of certain physical phenomena in the past creative period. But we humans might have been different had some other physical phenomena unfolded somewhere else in the distant past, such as a different beginning to the Universe than the Big Bang, or by our earth orbiting the sun at a different distance, thus affecting heat and cold and seasons, or the earth's being smaller in size than it is so that its gravity could not hold enough air for us, or any of a myriad of possibilities. Those other outcomes are just as valid as our present state and may well have existed in a wave form of possibilities and all could have collapsed as different particle forms in other universes, so maybe all of them came true also and all of the Universes so engendered are also existing simultaneously with this one. This means that we cannot look at ourselves and know completely who we are, nor can we say, with our limited vision, that this existence is all there is and the characteristics or achievements we have here are the only ones possible to us.

Does the Numinous Factor explain all this? Of course it does. The Numinous takes us out of the physical world that we can see and touch, and raises us to a contemplation of worlds beyond earthly reasoning and beyond materialism. Limitlessness frees us from the restriction of thinking that there can be only one Universe just because we do not yet have the power to fully sense or picture any more than that. Intuition gives us the power to conceive this realization through reception of information beyond what is generally understood by mortal rational processes. Continuity keeps us always focused on how we must throw off the limiting concept of Cause, and instead see everything as part of the constant Continuity that is ever existent. Energy reminds us that all is energy, and none of it is ever lost, so the outcomes of the waves of possibilities are never lost either. It means also that energy can transform or manifest itself in a wide variety of ways. And Unity reminds us that all possibilities are part of the great Whole, and that this Whole is far beyond our little human power to grasp, although we can certainly conceive of it through reception of Intuition.

The Direction of Time

Let us add another dimension to all of this. In our Newtonian world, there seems to be an arrow to the idea of time so that it seems to proceed in one direction only. If we drop a drinking glass, it seems to hit the floor and break. So far as we can see, that is a done deal and life proceeds from that point. There is no going back to do the thing over: The glass does not reassemble itself in a reverse arrow of time and jump back up into the table. This seems to be proof to people that events do cause each other and that things proceed in a direct line only, and that everything has to develop from where things are now. However, Limitlessness reminds us to expand our thinking a little bit and to look at the concept of time with an open mind.

The rules of physics do indeed allow the glass to reverse itself. As a symbol of this, if we film it falling, we can easily reverse the film and see it rising back into our hand again. It is just a matter of reversing the vector or direction of its travel. But the pieces? Can they be reversed? Well, when the glass hit the floor, the floor gave a little and the sudden stop caused fracturing along the crystal lines, but classical physics says that the floor could indeed reverse its give and instead pop the glass back up as all of the fractured pieces flew back together and became again a glass in our hand. It is just that there are so many pieces that would have to fly back together and fit exactly right that this one outcome is extremely unlikely. We just do not ever seem to see it because we see one or more of the huge number of other possible outcomes.

Time seems to be a warping in space based on gravity, as we will see in Einstein's view of outer space in the next section. In theory it could be seen as a thing, an entity, an entirety. If we could stand back and look from the viewpoint of the Numinous, time does not pass at all, but rather everything remains in an eternal present. Glass, pieces, and floor exist at the same instant, and the laws of physics can very well run in reverse because of the timeless present.

Obviously, the act of assuming that everything proceeds in linear fashion, so that once the electron has jumped or the glass has fallen, there is no turning back, could seem take away the totality of the Continuity of the Numinous by ignoring the other wave form possibilities of the glass (for example, falling and not breaking at all, or falling and cracking but maintaining integrity, or being caught at the last moment). It seems in our earthly view that the other possibilities just disappear and are lost. And yet we suspect that they do not and are allowed to play out their various outcomes in other universes.

One answer to all this could be in the functioning of the human consciousness. Nothing happens (in our estimation) unless we are aware of it. We may find out about it later, as in history, but we still have to have the knowledge of it. We apparently need to be consciously aware of a thing for it to have any reality for us. When we can conceive of it in our minds, it exists. If we are unconscious, we do not know anything is happening until someone brings it to our awareness when we wake up. Therefore, it is the concept in the awareness that gives reality. Now, in our *minds* we can go back and see many possible outcomes, such as the glass dropping and not breaking; as the glass cracking but remaining whole; as being saved by our making a desperate catch of it at ground level, and so forth. In fact, we can go back and replay the whole scenario as many times as we want, with a different outcome each time, and each outcome has reality for us since each exists in our minds. Therefore, each outcome lives, and time is merely replayed over and over. In our heads, then, we are timeless. At the end of all this, of course, the glass in its unbroken state remains in our minds, ready for another action in another scenario.

So let us put this into the concept of parallel universes. There is one universe in which the glass falls and is broken, and events for its owner and other people proceed from that point. There are others in which it falls, but is unbroken for any of a variety of circumstances. There are others in which it does a variety of other maneuvers or does not fall at all. The ramifications of such parallel universes in our own lives are staggering: the concept is that there are infinite universes in which we exist simultaneously due to the various paths and choices that we and others have already taken, and there are no lost possibilities. In one, you may make a decision one way and your life and the lives of others around you proceed from that point. In another, you make a different decision. In another, you make still a different one, and so it goes. Also, others make decisions that affect you in different ways. Every possible outcome can come to pass in the various parallel universes. This is the totality of the Continuity of the Numinous. If we just think that everything happens only once and in a linear fashion, this denies totality and puts us into the position of denying Limitlessness.

Simultaneity

After all, Limitlessness tells us that if space extends indefinitely, then there is room for more universes. Why the plural? Does not "Universe" describe all of outer space and the physical things in it? We remember that, until the twentieth century, even astronomers thought that the Universe consisted only of the Milky Way Galaxy in which we live because they could not see beyond it. But with today's telescopes, we can see billions of galaxies like ours, which should give us the hint that there could be billions more, or that there could be other universes with their own characteristics, rotating around their own centers with no relationship to this one. So in this book, we use the capitalized word "Universe" to refer to this physical entity made up of space and matter in which we exist, and which is probably vastly larger than the millions of light years across that we have measured so far. We will use the uncapitalized word "universes" to refer to any others that might exist, either in different locations, or with other characteristics, or even existing right next to us but containing the playing out of all the wave possibilities that are not realized in this one.

All this is rather staggering, but we can remember that, as various results of wave-particle collapse play out in other universes, happenings are not linear, but simultaneous. All possibilities can occur. They are not just physical, but are spiritual, which includes the physical. They are not separate, but linked, and everything is One. They are not caused, but come into being through Continuity, all of us being participants in the Creative act. And reality extends far beyond our normal four dimensions.

Note that it takes something like the Spiritual Factor to see all of this. We are trained to see the linear, one-way arrow of continuity. We are trained in our thinking processes and experiences in this life to see separateness, not Oneness. We accept without question the role of cause and even First Cause in life. And we cannot see beyond these four dimensions, and so we think that nothing else exists. It is through the application of the Numinous Factor or some similar one that we expand beyond these seeming constraints, instead seeing Oneness, seeing spirituality in all things, seeing Being instead of causing, and seeing that the most important thing we can do is achieve Enlightenment and a full realization of the Numinous and of our own Eternal Natures.

Growth and the Higgs Field

Now let us go back to the idea of growth in the linear, cause-and-effect side to our world. There certainly is growth, and the possible reason for our being here on earth is tied to it. Many people have long felt and written about the concept of our needing to grow spiritually as well as physically, mentally, and emotionally while living in this existence. The concept of physical growth of people, trees, even stars, is easy to see on the outside, but hard to grasp on the inside. To understand it, we have to bring back Energy and remember that Energy constitutes everything. The concept of mass is a convenient way to refer to a quantity of energy because through it, particles clump together into concrete forms that we can detect with our five senses and which are easier to understand than the concept of pure energy. Einstein related mass and energy in his famous equation: $E=mc^2$. This states that energy equals mass times the speed of light squared. Energy and mass are the same, but it is easier to see the growth of mass than that of energy.

We have already seen how the electromagnetic field with its photons and other particles extends throughout space, being very familiar to us in these days of radios, televisions, cell phones, and the Internet. The gravitational field with its gravitons also extends throughout space, but is less familiar to us because we have trouble grasping how it functions. Gravitons, the smallest units of gravity, are constantly in motion, with their waves and particles vibrating in a ceaseless flow of energy, creating gravity. But these are just two of the energy fields surrounding us.

As we would expect, there are other fields of energy. Let us look at just one of them: the Higgs Field, named after the Scottish physicist, Peter Higgs. It apparently was formed along with the Universe, but cooled off in the frigidity of space in an unusual way: It condensed into a non-zero value field throughout space. Note that it does have a value, and thus is not the zero-point field, the Electromagnetic Field. So it seems to have zero energy, but not zero value. According to models, its boson (a particle with a particular spin) will interact with another particle because of its non-zero value and will create a force between them, with the result that the other particle gains mass from the interaction. It seems to put a drag on the particle that allows it to gain volume as it plows through the field, much as how our leg muscles are increased when we run in soft sand. There are differences as to how this happens with simple, or with more complex particles, but for our spiritual search, the result is the same. Allowing particles to gain mass equates to their adding energy since mass itself is energy, as we know from the Principle of Energy. The particles then keep their energy because the Higgs Field exists everywhere and the particles cannot get away from it. In fact, if it were not for the Higgs Field, no particle in the Universe would have any mass at all.

Now, the trick with the Higgs Field is that this increase in mass or energy only occurs when particles are accelerating, not when they are floating freely. When particles increase their speed is when they are subject to the "drag" of the Higgs Field and are allowed to gain mass or energy. Going back to building muscle, we do not get much added mass when we are sitting around on the sand, but when we move through it and increase our effort, we gain the muscle.

It might well seem to the meditating observer that the spiritual side of this applies also. We humans have our own Higgs Field that imparts high energy to our spiritual natures, but only if we are accelerating, making an effort to grow in consciousness. If we are just floating along in life letting things happen to us, we do not gain spiritual strength or higher vibrations of energy. If we are accelerating, trying to increase our spirituality, we keep adding energy, and then more energy to that energy, and we rise in our levels of consciousness. The higher the energy we get, the greater the drag, and so the greater the energy we can get by overcoming this drag, maybe in an exponential function, where the curve rises more and more steeply the farther we go. This is a great example of the value of Intention in keeping us constantly pushing ourselves toward the goal of Enlightenment. Nothing causes anything, as we saw in Continuity, and so we are not out to accomplish anything on our own, but we are indeed taking advantage of the opportunity offered by the Numinous to allow our energies to increase and grow into a higher consciousness, gaining the experience that comes from overcoming obstacles, all as part of the Numinous manifesting through Continuity. This is worthy of some contemplation. Since scientists are now discovering the Higgs boson on the supercollider in Switzerland, we can expect more spiritual symbolism to arise from their discoveries.

Strings

The last thing we will look at in our short view of the Numinous in the quantum is the controversial Theory of Superstrings, a scientific theory that is still going through growing pains, but which, for the spiritual seeker, can show very well the operation of the Numinous as the most basic power in the Universe. The Theory is concerned with particles that are much smaller than anything we have been able to imagine, yet holds the promise of putting Newtonian physics, Einstein physics and quantum physics in balance by showing that all of their elements are basically made of the same stuff, which would be a huge breakthrough in the scientific world.

Atoms, as we know, are made up of protons, neutrons, and electrons. Protons and neutrons themselves are made up of quarks, and there are lots of other particles in the subatomic mix, such as nutrinos, gluons, taus, muons, and several more, with some people adding "morons" to the list for their own purposes. These particles are all arranged into family patterns when measured by mass, and are controlled by series of weak and strong forces that hold things in a delicate balance. Any unplanned changes in the masses of the particles or the strengths of the forces that control them, no matter how slight, would create chaos in the Universe as we know it. This is another aspect that lends credence to many people for the existence of an Intelligent Being in charge of Continuity: Not only is there an orderliness that random grouping would not have, but complete randomness would require these forces to change constantly in unpredictable ways, and they do not.

Many scientists now suggest that all of these subatomic particles are made up of loops that physicists call "strings," possibly one-dimensional or even zero-dimensional elements that vibrate. Their size is estimated to be one Planck length, or approximately 1.6×10^{-35} centimeters, too small to be seen or accurately measured at the moment. They do not break down any further because the key is not in the strings themselves, but in their vibrations. The different frequencies, amplitudes, patterns, harmonics, and maybe even intensities of their vibrations produce the great varieties of elements that we experience. That is to say, each different manifestation in this Universe is made up of vibrating strings that give resultant distinctive masses by movement through resistance as we saw in the Higgs Field. So instead of quarks, muons, taus, nutrinos, electrons, protons, atoms, molecules, bacteria, rocks, animals, trees, planets, stars and all the rest being made of different materials, they are all made of *the same stuff,* of strings, which are *all identical,* and vary from one another only by their vibration patterns, amplitudes, frequencies, and the like. It is these variations in vibration of the strings that give physical objects their individualities and their physical existence.

Let us apply the Factor to see a big ramification of all of this. The Principle of Energy reminds us that everything is energy, and that mass is only a way of describing it. Energy consists of vibrations, not substance, and so energy is the basis of all that is. Limitlessness tells us to expand our limited thinking beyond what seems to be, and Unity reminds us that the Numinous is present everywhere. Let us then ask the question: "If these strings are the most elemental things that exist and there is nothing smaller or more fundamental than they are, what keeps all these strings vibrating in just these specific ways with no variations, giving identity, mass, and existence to everything on a continuing basis?"

Maybe it is the Numinous.

We remember that the Numinous is not a separate Being but is the substance of all that is, being the most fundamental aspect of all existence. That is Its Essence, as we saw at the beginning of the book, making up everything that exists rather than being a separate Being that moves things about. It is, therefore, at the basis of everything throughout the Universe. The Numinous is Omnipresent, as we saw in the first chapter, and so is the fundamental Energy at the core of every aspect of continuity. All existing entities, including humans, are different manifestations of that same Energy and the Numinous is the basic essence of them all. The Numinous, then, is indeed the only energy source and is at the basis of everything that exists, imparting to each string its correct vibration to maintain its identity, and also keeps bringing forth new manifestations as a natural function of Continuity. This is the Numinous, the totally awesome One.

So, instead of thinking of sun, moon, and stars as different masses, we can think of them as different manifestations of Energy. If we see people as manifestations of the same Energy, we can identify with them in oneness, as in Unity and Limitlessness. We can identify with everything just by seeing in it the Numinous, the basic spirituality that makes up everything. We can therefore have confidence and happiness in knowing that the Numinous is who we are and is in control of all life here and whatever is in the plane of existence that we will go to next. We are not left here alone and in a panic.

Multiple Dimensions

Now, let us look at Limitlessness for another aspect of all of this. One of the most fascinating aspects of the string theory is that its equations only work in nine dimensions, rather than just the three with which we are very familiar. When the dimension of time is added, there are ten. Scientists have tried to picture these extra dimensions as tiny, curled-up spheres at every point along the normal three dimensions, and math models seem to indicate this, but it is still all rather unsatisfactory and does not concern us here anyway since there is another way that these dimensions can exist, and we will look at it. We will not be concerned with other sub-theories that speak of other numbers of dimensions because the spiritual aspect would be the same. We will just look at the ten dimensions of the String Theory.

We can get a better idea of how these dimensions exist by thinking of people whom we know. We can see them in the normal three physical dimensions and we can watch time pass for them, making four dimensions, but we cannot see their mental dimensions, which could be three, or their emotional ones, which could be three more, for a total of ten. We know that those dimensions exist and are right there next to us as part of the person, but we cannot see six out of their ten. We can sense their effects, in a vague way, by how the person acts or talks, or by putting EEG sensors on their head that show brain waves being generated, but we cannot actually enter into the mind or heart of anyone else. The only way to know someone is to be them, which is impossible in this earthly existence. So it is that other dimensions might be right next to us, but we cannot see them except by getting ideas of them in our minds. When we use Limitlessness, we can expand ourselves enough to sense these dimensions, and therefore increase our knowledge through the Numinous.

Let us see why this is so. String theory now indicates that some strings are open (meaning that the loose ends are free) and some are closed in a complete loop. The ends of open strings are actually limited by, or even fastened to, the multi-dimensional frameworks called "branes," in which they exist, and so they can move around inside their branes but not move outside of them. Closed strings are independent, not limited by branes, and so can move around among various dimensions. It turns out that photons, the smallest particles of light and the units by which we visually sense everything, are open strings, and thus are contained within this three-dimensional world or brane in which we all seem to exist because it is all we can see by means of the light photons around us. This means that they not only render this brane invisible to us (since they can travel anywhere inside it and there is no contrast by which we can distinguish it, much like a whiteout in a snowstorm), but also that they cannot travel to any other dimensions, and so we cannot see or measure those other dimensions. They might be located right next to us, as we have already realized, but we cannot detect them. However, we can grasp them in our thoughts, so thoughts must be closed strings, able to travel anywhere, and this is a critical part of our ability to overcome limits and soar free.

Now, only one of the messenger particles that we know of is made of closed-loop strings, and that is the graviton, able to travel anywhere. Since the graviton is an attractive force, it could be that our thoughts are related to gravitons. Even here on earth, many people say that the things you think about are attracted to you, and if you want good things in life, just set your intention on them and they will have the ability and openness to flow to you. Perhaps the graviton plays a role in this. After all, we can conceive of things that we cannot see, which sometimes forms a big part of artistic creativity. Through Limitlessness, we can accomplish the same thing metaphysically. It is worthy of contemplation.

All of this means that we humans, for example, are at least ten-dimensional entities, of far greater complexity than we or even scientific theory can picture at the moment. But there is even one more dimension to think about, related to the scientific observation that there seem to be at least five string theories. To unite the five, an eleventh dimension has been proposed, one that takes into account the peaks and valleys of the others and unites them into one. If so, then we humans are actually entities of eleven dimensions, which shows us to be even more complex than we might have thought in our limited, physical ways, and makes most of our worrying about what will happen to us after death a moot point because we cannot fathom the totality of who we really are right now.

Let us contemplate this. If we are living in many different universes, the fact that the body we occupy in this one ceases to function and dies does not mean that we have died in any other universe. Our basic entity may go on living for a very long time in many different universes, having many different experiences. Also, since we do not know most of our dimensions, how can we insist on keeping these particular ones after we die? We are much more complex that we ourselves realize, so why limit ourselves trying to keep this personality and body with which we are familiar when there may be much better ones if we see our fullness. The fact that we ultimately are all One within the Numinous, which we can see through applying all five of the Principles, can give us great contentment knowing that all is under control and we are never lost or cut off, but rather are whole and complete in the Wholeness and Completeness of the Numinous. Death, therefore, has no terror for us, since we are multi-faceted manifestations of Spirituality that is a part of us and is the totality of everything.

This, then, has been a look at how the Numinous functions at the subatomic level. To further expand our consciousness, let us now look at some ways that allow the Numinous to be seen in the physics of outer space, bearing in mind always that all of the massive bodies we see out there are still made up of the subatomic components that we have seen in this chapter, and thus are still Numinous in their basic natures.

CHAPTER NINE

• • • • • • • •

The Factor and the Cosmos

Scientific Theories of the Universe

Now, let us see how the Spirituality Factor works with some of the physics of outer space. One of the biggest questions to vex mankind throughout the ages has been: Where did this earth come from? We will look at some scientific ideas about this on a large scale, and then will apply the Factor to see where spirituality takes us.

To the ancients here on earth, the skies seemed to remain in an unchanging state. The stars all stayed in the same patterns year to year, so much so that they were made into pictures, and myths were created about them. Of course, there were a few that seemed to wander, but these were called "planets," from the Greek word for "wanderer," and as time went on, they were seen as being different, unable to shine on their own, and thus not stars. And there were a few meteors and comets to mix things up, but generally the universe was seen as stable and unchanging. And, of course, the earth was thought to be flat, with the sky an arched dome overhead and the domain of Deity somewhere on the other side of that. This was the viewpoint of many early religious writers.

We saw earlier that, until early in the last century, even scientists thought that the Universe consisted only of our own Milky Way Galaxy. All this changed in the 1920s when telescopes became more powerful, at which point not just more stars came into view, but whole galaxies, each made up of possibly billions of stars. A couple of these galaxies had been somewhat visible previously without a telescope, appearing as fuzzy patches, but there was little knowledge about what they really were. Nowadays, we see beautiful photos of galaxies with spiraling arms of stellar dust and with red, yellow, and blue stars rotating around a center that is densely packed with even more stars. Astronomers keep discovering more and more of them until there are now billions of such known galaxies, so many that we have not yet had the time to get to know most of them.

Edwin Hubble, for whom the wonderful space telescope is named, and others began analyzing the light from these galaxies through a spectrometer, a device that measures the aspects of their light. As we saw earlier, white light breaks down into colors when passed through a prism, and a rainbow's colors come from breaking sunlight into those same familiar colors through raindrops acting like prisms. Glowing materials give different bands of colors when their emissions are passed through a spectrometer, which functions somewhat like a prism. Well, Hubble discovered that the light from the newly-discovered galaxies was shifted slightly more toward the lower frequencies than would have been expected. Scientists referred to this as a red-shift because the infrared frequencies are lower than those of observable light. It became obvious that the Doppler Effect was in play here.

The Doppler Effect

What is the Doppler Effect? If you stand by railroad tracks as a train approaches blowing its horn, the pitch of the horn will be higher as it comes toward you, and will drop to a lower pitch as it passes and goes away from you. This is because the frequencies of the sound waves are crowded together by the train's forward speed as it comes toward you, thus giving them a shorter wavelength and a higher pitch, and then are stretched out slightly as the train recedes from you, giving them a lower pitch. The same thing can happen with the light of the stars, and when measurements were taken of the newly-found galaxies, it was discovered that all of them had the red-shift, with light spectra shifted slightly to the lower frequencies, indicating that probably they are all moving away from us just as the train does when its pitch drops. One says "probably," because red-shift can result from other things, such as the pull on light's photons by extreme gravity, but the general conclusion seems to be that the Universe is expanding and is not static. These measurements have been repeated throughout the ensuing years with other galaxies as they have been discovered and the results have been the same, except for a few that are very close to us where other factors come into play.

So the Universe is expanding. And since we now know, as the ancients did not, that we on earth are not at the center of even the Milky Way Galaxy, much less at the center of the Universe, we would expect that the galaxies would all be rushing away from each other, not just from us, and indeed they are. Everything is moving away from everything else. Furthermore, their trajectories seem to indicate that they are all receding from a central point, and thus came the Big Bang Theory of the formation of the Universe, the idea that it all started from a super explosion billions of years ago, and that everything is still expanding from that starting point out into deeper space.

Actually, this had been predicted mathematically by Einstein early in the twentieth century when he applied the equations of his General Theory of Relativity to the Universe, and found that the equations would not apply if the Universe were static; it had to be growing larger or smaller. He tried to introduce a Constant to get rid of this effect, since at his time everyone assumed that the Universe was unchanging, but his original equations were correct, and it is reported that he later regretted making this change.

The Big Bang

"The Big Bang Theory" was a derisive term applied to the concept of an explosive origin of the Universe by an astrophysicist who did not even believe in it, but the name stuck. It postulates that this Universe, meaning all the billions of galaxies, each with easily billions of stars, was all concentrated in one spot some fourteen billion years ago, with such intense heat, internal pressures, and gravitational problems that it just blew up. Now, that sounds simple to understand, but physicists have also found that it expanded so rapidly to avoid collapsing back down that the expansion would have had to exceed by far the speed of light, and such speed is considered impossible. So another corollary was put into place: The universe expanded outward with such force and speed that it took space and time along with it. In our experience, the speed of light is related to fixed time. But if time itself is expanding, then there is no limit or measurement of light's speed. Apparently, galaxies are still rushing away from each other, maybe even accelerating, and also not necessarily traveling through space that already exists, in the view of some scientists, but are possibly stretching space as they move. This is called "inflation," and it opens up an interesting question: "Did time and space only start with the creation of this Universe?"

If it did, then nothing existed before the Big Bang, either as matter or in the passage of time. There would have been nothing existing outside of the space into which the Universe expanded; there would have been no existence before the Bang; and there would be no other universes now. But all this limits the Numinous to just this Universe and just this one ongoing act of Creativity, and Limitlessness shows that we cannot limit the Numinous this way, nor can we restrict the concept of Creation.

Let us take a minute to look back at a couple of patterns. As we saw earlier, electrons circle the nuclei of atoms just as our planets revolve around the sun just as the sun and other stars revolve around the center of the Milky Way just as the stars of other galaxies that we can see revolve around their centers. This is a pattern that repeats at various levels of nature, and can repeat in outer space as well.

Well, we could say that the expansion of all the red-shift galaxies seems to break that pattern, but let us look at another one. Just as particles spring into life in the Electromagnetic belt and then fade back into the soup, just as plants spring into life and growth and then die away back into the earth, just as stars come to life and grow as nuclear fusion begins in a condensing dust cloud and then either expand greatly or collapse when their fuel is spent, so galaxies can spring into life, grow and expand (as the ones we see are doing), and then decay back down to where they can begin the cycle anew. To put these two patterns together, it is quite possible that this entire Universe, still expanding, is circling the center of some vast cloud of other universes that itself has electromagnetic clouds of particles that come into being, expand, and collapse again. There is nothing new or startling about this concept except for its scale, and scale is of no effect on the Numinous. We just have to use Limitlessness and Intuition to escape the restrictions of our own thinking and experience.

By the way, we note that our sun is only about five billion years old, and that this Universe existed for billions of years before the sun was finally created, and then the earth with its somewhat intelligent beings (us) came well after that. This seems to cast doubt on the theory of some people that the whole Universe was created just to give birth to the human race.

Anyway, there is no problem in using Intuition, Limitlessness, and Continuity to envision space in which universes can explode into being, grow as their stars and galaxies are continually formed and nuclear processes instigated with everything being based on entities rotating around centers, and then all of it condense back down and die away as others explode into being in other areas. The Numinous and space are infinite and there is plenty of room. And when we add in Energy, we see that nothing is actually created or destroyed because all is energy, and so all is recycled over and over in different forms. Again, we think of the Hebrew word "organized." Then let us add in Unity, which shows that all of this is unified into One, the vastness of the Numinous that goes beyond our little attempts to define Deity. There is no end of any of it, and this can boggle the mind as we limited humans seek to conceive of it unless we see it as all spiritual and ourselves as a part of the spiritual and thus one together in the Completeness and Totality of All that Is.

The Aspect of Time

Now let us look again at the time aspect. We are accustomed to the earthly way of measuring time as the interval between two events that happen at successive points along a timeline. Thus we call our concept "linear time." That is, if one event happens, and then another clearly happens subsequent to it, we place them in successive points along a line going from past to present. We also note the length of the interval along this timeline by counting some sort of elapsed pulses or ticks and, when we compare these to the ticks of another succession of events, we say that one series is longer or shorter than the other series, and thus more or less time elapses. But this all depends on our choice of the yardstick of comparison.

Actually, there is another way of seeing it. Time is a dimension. Our familiar three dimensions of length, width, and height can be combined with time to make a four-dimensional figure called "spacetime." The four dimensions are therefore inseparable. The size of an object, for example, can vary according to its speed in relation to the speed of an observer because their coordinating or orientation systems change constantly. This can be laid out on maps and calculated. And speed is involved in everything that exists. Even we humans are constantly in motion, even when we think we are at rest. How? Not only are the atoms in constant motion inside of us, but the earth we inhabit is rotating; it is also orbiting the sun; the sun is rushing along orbiting its center in the Milky Way Galaxy; and the galaxy itself is in motion as it races away from all other galaxies in the Universe, and who knows what motions the Universe itself is involved in as part of the orbit of a greater system! We are carried along in all of these vectors of varying speeds and directions without sensing it. It is a little like the teacups at Disneyland, where there are many vectors of movement in play all at once in different directions, so that we may seem to be standing still at one point, and then be hurtling at high G's at another. So we and everything else are in a plethora of different times, dimensions, speeds, and directions continuously.

Again, this can be laid out on maps and calculated. It is intriguing to think that the future may well exist as part of spacetime, since Einstein has indicated that time is really a warp on the fabric of space. After all, the Numinous cannot have O3 if there are things in the future that It does not yet know or of which It is not a part or of which It is not the inherent moving power. Intuition, Continuity, and Limitlessness show us this. Our mental block is in thinking of time as linear, with one thing happening after another, and, therefore, with some of these events still in the future and unable to be seen. Actually, the Numinous has the complete picture because of having all knowledge through Omniscience. It is easier to think of everything as being timeless, but actually everything might be in an eternal present, within which everything exists with time as one of the dimensions involved, such as length or width. However, like the blindfolded men describing the elephant, we see only a little bit here and another little bit there. Everyone's spacetime has a slightly different aspect than anyone else's, but when they are all added up, they make a totality, a oneness, an eternal present. As Enlightenment grows, we will tend to see more and more as a unity, especially through the Principles of Intuition and Unity.

We can also try to say, through our human limitations, that because time seems to be linear, then time is just the one-way arrow that we saw earlier, as shown by the glass that we saw fall and break, a situation that seems irreversible. But let us apply Intuition and Limitlessness again and remember that this is only one way for the wave of possibilities to collapse into a particle form. We saw that there can be other ways. Since the Numinous is timeless, we might suspect that all of these possible outcomes already exist, all at the same instant, and so could be seen in their entirety right now if we had the overall view.

It is a little like how we see the light arriving from a distant galaxy that might be millions of light years away (a light year being the distance that light travels in a year or roughly six trillion miles). The light we are seeing actually left its galaxy millions of years ago, and we are seeing the galaxy as it was then, not necessarily how it is now, if it even still exists. Well, if we had the ability to put ourselves out there in space close enough to it, we would see the light that was only a thousand years old, or even one year old if we were close enough, but would we still be seeing it as it actually is today? Probably we would not, because our time would shift somewhat in our act of moving toward it. All states of time exist simultaneously, and could be seen all at once if timespace were laid out on a map as part of Continuity and Unity. We could even see the "future," according to our timeframe. That area of spacetime also exists because what galaxies are now is what we would see in our future as their light reached us a few billion years in our future, but it actually exists in the present. Their "future" (to us), then, is already out there traveling through space, and if we could put ourselves along its line, we could see it while it was still "future" to people on earth. So past, present, and future all exist at the same time as part of Unity and Continuity, and it is only our view of time as a linearity and our insistence on seeing things as "caused" by something else that keep us from experiencing all of this. And this is still just one part of the overall nature of the Numinous. By the way, we would not age much on our trip to the far galaxy because all our processes would slow down due to our high speed, according to Einstein's Theories, and so we could see the future while being still nearly the same age as on earth.

The Timeless Present

Everything in the Universe, then, is in a timeless present. All of the possibilities are contained in the Oneness, just as quantum waves carry all possibilities that can collapse into different particles at a later "time" according to our eyes, since the particle forms are really all one in the present because the wave form contains all their possibilities. Again, the block to our being able to see this lies in our thinking of time as linear. It is related to our habit seeing "cause" in things, but Continuity shows us that we have only a limited view and we like to think that one event causes another when actually all events are happening in a simultaneous way as part of the ongoing Continuity of the Numinous. We see a succession of events, and we assume that one causes the next and that time elapses in between them, whereas Individual events really are only a part of a Whole that already exists, just as the whole of Electricity has been here all along. We see it in a linear fashion, one discovery after another in what we see as passage of time. If we saw it in a non-linear way, it would all be there and no time would pass during our discovery.

Therefore, time might be seen as an illusion based on our limited viewpoint, as Limitlessness will show us when we are able to use different criteria to experience it. When we can free ourselves from words, rules, limitations, and the narrow earthly views of the physical, we will see a bigger view. It does us no good to use earthly words such as timelessness because the true concept is in a different plane that we cannot see strictly through rational thought. It is a little like trying to see infrared and ultraviolet with our eyes: The waves are there and can enter our eyes, possibly damaging them, but we cannot see them unaided and we did not even have the concept of them in the first place until they were discovered by other means. So we have to go beyond regular physical phenomena to comprehend more of what is there. We can use Limitlessness to remind ourselves of that, and then Unity and Continuity to see the operation, letting Intuition fill in the areas where our rational processes try to get in the way.

Speaking of using different means, different people could travel through the solar system in distinct ways and would see it from varying angles. The patterns of stars would differ according to the different possible trajectories. Also, one person traveling at high speed would experience one passage of time; another at a slower pace would have a different time experience and thus a different physical presentation because of the different developments of galactic material over his sensing of what he calls linear time, even when covering the same route. Timespace would warp differently in different areas, and would be different for distinct observers. And even events seen simultaneously by different observers would have a different timespace for each because each observer would be on a different path and trajectory and velocity from the others. We could again draw the corollary that each of us on earth is on a different path of life, and we will all see things differently from what others see due to our personal differences. But we are all still one in the overall view. Just as scientists measuring a great number of individual possibilities in the quantum world can still find enough general agreement among them that they can draw accurate conclusions, we can say that people are pretty much the same even though they seem to be quite different. There is a timeless wholeness in people when they are taken in a generality because the Numinous is timeless, and is in and as everything, but we humans seem limited to taking things individually and measuring time in a linear fashion in our worldly doings.

This shows that we are on thin ice if we try to explain one aspect of physics or of the Universe without being able to explain all of them within Unity, because everything is interconnected into One. It is a little like a physician who uses considerable skill in treating one disorder, but does not treat the whole body as one, so other side effects or disorders crop up. If the whole body were seen as one unit holistically, treatments might be far different.

So Einsteinian physics, the physics of outer space that we looked at earlier, seems to indicate that time is a curve or warp that bends back onto itself, and that our three dimensions plus time make the four-dimensional entity called "spacetime" with nothing existing outside of it. But applying the principles of the Numinous Factor shows that there is indeed something "outside" of it because the Numinous is not limited to this Universe, as we have seen. Our thoughts are not limited either, and neither are the types of universes that we can envision as one way in which we participate in the Creative Continuum. After all, we live in a certain atmosphere with life based on carbon and oxygen, and we think that this is the only way to exist. But Limitlessness and Intuition indicate that other universes exist, possibly based on different elements and methods of formation, and each would have its own timespace. Recalling the scientists feeding arsenic to the bacteria, we remember not to limit our thinking or spiritual receptivity.

After all, Energy reminds us that everything is energy. The vast Energy that is the Numinous spreads out and fills all spacetime, taking many forms and changing constantly as particles or stars are born, exist, and then die back to leave space and material for others to form. Let us remember, too, that our thoughts are like that: forming, rising to our consciousness, and then fading away to be replaced with others. These thoughts are one of the means by which we can comprehend the Continuity and the various entities within it. Enlightenment is another, so we turn to EMILY along with LUCIE to perceive clearly.

This whole subject seems to be as big as spacetime itself, so let us take this discussion back to the Big Bang Theory.

CHAPTER TEN

- - - - - - - -

Formations and Cycles

Timing of the Big Bang

Scientists can envision what happened a thousandth of a second (in our time), then a hundredth of a second, then a tenth of a second after the initial Big Bang, with the tremendous cooling and expansion that occurred even within that short period, and then they go on to the first minute, and then half-hour, with descriptions of every step in the formation of the Universe as we know it, with complex interactions taking place among particles and forces as the extremely hot temperatures began to cool down and physical actions began to take place. This is interesting if we back up and think about it, because scientists also indicate that time could not have been passing at this point since time and space were being carried along with the expansion. We will see more on this later.

Scientists explain that the Universe itself, as we are aware of it, did not start to take form until one or two million years after the initial explosion, and although it is still expanding even now, and possibly even accelerating, it could arrive at a point where it begins to condense again. This latter possibility is referred to as the Big Crunch, as opposed to the

Big Bang, and there is considerable argument as to whether it really could take place. If the Universe is expanding rapidly enough, expansion can go forever, say some scientists. If it slows down enough, it can be pulled back together by gravity, say others. If it does something in between, the results are uncertain. Limitlessness and Continuity show us that there can easily be similarities between the Universe and a simple particle in the Electromagnetic Field: As we have seen, something pops into existence in each, grows, exerts influence, and then dies back to become part of the "soup" again. There is a difference in scale, of course, and in the amount of "time" that elapses, but the principle is the same. When we apply the Numinous to it, the likelihood exists that eventually there will be a Big Crunch or Big Collapse because that is a logical continuation of the cyclic aspects of Continuity. The central problem is that expansion and contraction are related to the passage of time, and if time varies because of aspects of the space warp, different readings could be experienced.

In the Big Picture, the timing and complexity of these things also may seem to depend on the amount of matter that is present, since matter (or energy) is what exerts gravitational pull through the gravitons. On the other hand, we saw that the subatomic world is just as complex, with great amounts of matter; with strong, weak, and gravitational forces interacting; and with constant activity and change. We remember that, regardless of the sizes of the universes and galaxies that we see, their elemental materials are still based on the tiny, subatomic world with all of its forces and complexities. So everything is only a matter of degree. Unity reminds us that the subatomic and outer space worlds are still all one, and function along the same proportionate lines, so there really is nothing that would impede this Universe from collapsing back and starting again as something else. Since this is all part of the operations of the Numinous and since we all are Numinous, we are a part of the cyclical nature of the Universe, which we can see when we drop our limitations of thinking through Limitlessness and Intuition.

Dark Matter and Wobbles

Let us return to dark matter and dark energy. Observations show that stars in our Milky Way galaxy do not circle the center in flat planes like the particles that form the rings of Saturn, but instead move up and down a little. Now, Newton's laws indicate that a body in motion tends to remain in motion in a straight line unless something acts upon it to change its direction, so if we can apply Newtonian physics to outer space, which is risky, it seems that, in addition to the dense center of the galaxy that keeps the stars circling it, there are also masses of matter out there, attracting stars and giving them the propensity to wobble. Also, it seems that the rotational speeds of the stars around the center of the galaxy are the same, rather than varying individually, which could indicate that they are part of a large body of dark matter that is carrying them along. We do not know for sure because we cannot see this body or understand it. But the Numinous has understood it and *is* it by the very nature of the Omniconstant that we saw earlier. In addition, we do not have to worry about where this dark matter came from because Continuity reminds us that it rises directly and continuously from the Numinous without any cause. Of course, all is energy, as the Principle of Energy reminds us, and the Numinous is all the energy that is, so we see again that our efforts to understand are quite feeble if we try to leave spirituality out of our calculations.

Since everything is just energy, then dark matter and dark energy are really the same, but apparently the gravitational aspects of the masses of dark matter lead to slightly different operations for the two. This aspect decreases even further our ability to set limits on the Creation through pure science. Therefore, we can put dark matter, dark energy, parallel universes and extended dimensions into the category of things we can conceive of through Intuition, Limitlessness, and Continuity, knowing that, for now, none of this can be understood without awareness of the Numinous.

However, Limitlessness and Intuition remind us of our earlier observation that if we do enough calculations in the quantum world using equations that may be only forty percent accurate, we still will come up with a good general idea. After all, Energy reminds us that energy is energy wherever it is found, and Limitlessness, Unity, and Continuity remind us that that our work with the complexities of the subatomic world still equate well with those of outer space even though we know little about either. All of this certainly indicates the Presence of the Numinous as the Aspect that actually exists as all of this is due to Omnipresence; knows all of this in detail due to Omniscience; and keeps it together and running due to Omnipotence, letting us see these principles through Intuition.

According to the Big Bang Theory, interactions, over time, were able to take place as expansion and cooling occurred, so that various atoms were formed, gradually creating the different elements that we know. Hydrogen and helium, the simplest elements, make up the vast majority of the so-called matter of the Universe and were formed early in the process. We have already seen how the heavier elements needed for life as we know it, such as oxygen, nitrogen, carbon, and iron, were formed later and wound up in such places as our earth. (As we saw before, is it not thought-provoking to look at your own hand and realize that the carbon atoms in it came from the center of a massive star that exploded billions of years ago?) All this is cumbersome, takes many years to happen, and covers a vast amount of space.

So now we have stars growing and exploding, using hydrogen and helium for their violent nuclear processes, and constantly changing their different elements. We have vast numbers of planets being created, and evolving as ours did. We have enormous amounts of matter and energy interacting, as well as specific fields, both far out in space and also all around us that we are rapidly learning how to identify and deal with. As we can see, there is a lot for our Numinous Factor to handle, but Energy really helps, since everything is just energy and the Numinous is all the energy.

Defining a Universe

"If a tree falls in a forest without anyone around, does it make a sound?" This question has instigated long and heated arguments, but the answer is so simple that it eludes people. It is: What is your definition of "sound?" If your definition means waves in the air, then there is indeed sound, but if your definition means the effect sensed by a person as these waves hit a human's eardrums, then there is no sound. So it is with definitions of this Universe. One is that the word "Universe" is the sum total of everything we can perceive in what surrounds us. But there is much around us that we cannot see well enough yet to calculate if it is part of the cohesive structure of galaxies that were formed in our Big Bang and are still interacting with each other as they expand, giving direction and relationship in a unity that was formed at our beginning, or galaxies that have nothing to do with our entity and are interacting in an organized way with another huge entity past our boundaries. There may well be elements farther out than we can yet see that form multiple universes, meaning entities that may well exist in completely different planes, dimensions, spiritual consciousnesses, and may be of different core principles, chemicals, or time warps, having been formed in very different ways that give them distinctive characteristics. Once we define a term, the definition sets it apart from other terms, so by using the term "Universe," are we talking about what we can see and measure in our ways, or are we referring to all the creations of the Numinous that may well exist in other ways? Defining something sets up a way of looking at it, and by its nature sets limits, so we must be leery about defining things too quickly and saying that other universes do not exist.

Actually, as we saw earlier, a fish does not define water. He does not even know he is in that medium. It is just part of his existence. Similarly, the hidden definitions of things that we carry around with us are so much a part of our earthly thinking that we may not even recognize their effects on us. Can we be completely impartial? No, we cannot. We function from complex viewpoints that have been built into us over the years. Many of our outlooks come from ideas that were placed in our minds by others so long ago that we know of no other way to think, and we accept these ideas without question, so we function like the fish, not really knowing the medium in which we operate. This means that we should ask ourselves: How are we approaching the materials in this book?

If we accept the word "Universe" as meaning all there is, then we have set exclusion boundaries based on limited acquaintanceship, and we are closed to many possible insights of interrelated entities. If we decide, through becoming aware of Limitlessness and Intuition, to accept this Universe as one in many, we can expand, but we still have boundaries. If we can accept everything in total as the work of the Numinous and do not even see separate universes in the first place, we may not be setting any more boundaries, but the concepts that then arise might seem to go beyond human comprehension. That is where the Enlightenment phase of the Numinous comes in, releasing us from our thinking and reasoning and, instead, letting us set up awareness that allows intuitive thoughts to be recognized by our spiritual centers, bringing larger truths than reasoning power alone can furnish.

These truths can be different for different people, but that is actually the nature of the quantum, as we have seen. The larger truth is that people who aspire to spiritual understanding tend to operate at a higher level of consciousness than those who are at other levels of understanding, and this might be more valuable to some people than increased specific scientific knowledge. Science is, of course, vitally necessary, and to obtain scientific knowledge through rational thinking, we can consult great numbers of books and Internet articles on the subject. In this book, we just try to establish a different mode of approach that can apply to a great number of questions about the world in which we live. We speak here more of methodology than of specific fact.

As an example, we have seen how our Universe combines our three dimensions plus time into spacetime, a four-dimensional aspect of Einstein's General Theory of Relativity. It is thought of as a structure, like a rubber sheet that can stretch and flex around in a circle. However, as we have seen, string theory operates in at least eleven dimensions, leaving seven dimensions outside of what we can envision. It is now evident that there are extra space dimensions and even time dimensions (since time is so flexible) outside of our logical understanding and reasoning power, and that these other dimensions are part of the Numinous. Other time dimensions could account for the questions of what has been happening before and during the Big Bang, since these dimensions could also be right next to us, or could be outside the framework of our particular Universe. We do not know with our reasoning power. The easiest way to explain how we are aware of such things is by saying that our thoughts can travel outside of this brane, bringing us added information from outside that we would be able to see with light, but light is stuck here. However, we remember that the Numinous is all there is and so our thoughts are part of the Omniscience of the Numinous in the first place. When we insist on using only our reasoning power (which is also of the Numinous, of course) and insist on leaving Spirituality out of it, we are operating on a lower level of consciousness than when we recognize the Numinous and therefore see dimensions more clearly.

Linking

Another way of sensing things in other dimensions is through linking. We have seen how, in the quantum world, a particle can be born with a spin that instantly allows an effect on the spin of another particle some distance away. This happens too fast to be a result of direct influence because that would mean that the influence, whatever it is, would have to travel faster than the speed of light, which is impossible. But it can happen when both are of the same body, so that the continuity of the body causes this influence on each at the same time. Continuity reminds us that nothing causes anything, and all is a result of the infinitely varied manifestations of the Numinous. Well, one way in which we can be aware of other dimensions is through the linking from our being part of the Numinous. All we have to do is open our awareness to It and we are linked to Intuitions that can give us this knowledge.

The caution still is that we cannot do this just with our earthly personalities or egos. The ego is set up to guide us through this materialistic existence and give us an earthly personality, but it does not function in spiritual things. The only way we can be truly Enlightened and see the Numinous as Everything is to let the ego, the self, fall away, and let our spiritual center, our Self, be revealed as our identity. Even though the self is part of the Numinous, it is the Self that is in constant contact with the Numinous as the spiritual side of our existence, and is our true personality. The earthly personality, the self, is made up of things that are of only limited, temporal value.

Using physical knowledge without taking into consideration the spiritual can be like looking at a common-looking rock and not seeing the lovely crystals of a geode within it. We could use that example and say that we have to disregard outward appearances in order to seek the beauty within just as we look within a physical person to see their spiritual nature and positive values. The geologist can take one step further and see the beauty in all sorts of rocks, not just geodes, appreciating the value of each. We can do the same, and sense the latent power and spiritual nature of each rock, regardless of what it looks like, sensing its possible role in other areas of the galaxy, and maybe its role in other solar systems over the billions of years of evolution of our Universe. The spiritual observer can actually identify with the rock in oneness and appreciate how both are part of the continual Continuity of the Numinous. Can we see how the Principles of the Factor operate here? Continuity says that nothing causes anything and that everything comes from the infinite facets of the Numinous. Limitlessness reminds us to expand ourselves beyond normal restrictions of human thinking and feeling to realize greater things. Unity stresses the oneness of everything, including that of humans with rocks. Intuition gives us the insight to see the Numinous in everything that is, and Energy points out that the Numinous is the totality of the energy of the Universe, and that the rock is as much a part of Energy as we are.

Other Powers

This takes us to other aspects of power. A great deal of study has gone into dark holes. We now know that they are areas of extreme density of matter, whose gravity pull is so strong that not even light can escape. So there are forces operating that we cannot even see, much less understand, and this bespeaks the Numinous, which is in the dark holes just as much as elsewhere and controls them by being a part of them beyond our capacity to understand right now.

We also have seen that gravity itself is a power. We do not yet understand it, and we certainly have not yet seen the graviton, its smallest particle, although we do know many of its effects and can calculate them to some degree. But gravity has one aspect that is still beyond us. As we saw earlier, the graviton is apparently a closed-loop string, unlike light which is an open-loop string and therefore stays stuck to the three-dimensional walls of its brane here on earth. The graviton is free to travel, and thus can penetrate other dimensions and universes, possibly supplying a messenger service of a sort and maybe allowing other effects to arise that we cannot even imagine. Since there is order and intelligence in the Universe rather than chaos, the graviton could be a unifying factor in its far-flung journeys. After all, it is an attractive power.

We remember the Higgs Field and the way its spiritual component may allow us to gain spiritual mass as we accelerate through its drag just as physical particles gain mass from its effects. The spiritual components of particles such as the graviton may well have strengths alongside the purely physical ones since everything is spiritual at its base and there is no such thing as something purely physical. We also remember how the Higgs Field boson, the smallest particle of its Non-Zero Field, gives mass to everything. Scientists are now finding evidence of the boson on the new supercollider in Switzerland, but even so, we are still very far from understanding how the Higgs Field gives everything the mass that makes them visible or detectable to us by imparting qualities and characteristics to them. Yet the metaphysician can see right away how the basic spiritual nature of the Higgs Field could also impart spiritual mass to us for our growth to higher consciousness.

If this can be taken as so, then it calls to mind the claim by some that we can attract whatever we want by just thinking about it. They say that the Universe says "yes" to whatever idea we plant in it. Others say that there is no evidence of this in any kind of statistical examination, and that it could lead to unforeseen problems. After all, if everyone on the earth planted the thought of obtaining a million dollars and received it, the money would then be worthless because of the oversupply. Well, discussion of the possible spiritual effects of the graviton indicates that there might be a middle ground between these views. If thoughts are actually things, as many contend, then they can be acted upon by gravity. Thoughts would be extraordinarily light, of course, but a single graviton also exerts a very tiny force. So the possibility exists of dealing in intention or suggestion, rather than direct, overt action for an attractive force to be present. An idea planted has an intention and thus allows a particular collapse of a wave form to take place. It is subtle, but there could be an attractive force involved.

The fact that the graviton can travel freely, being a closed-loop string, also raises the idea of how we can imagine or be aware of other dimensions or universes that we cannot see. Since light is limited to this three-dimensional brane, we cannot see anything else. But the graviton can carry the attractive power of our thoughts to and from other dimensions and universes, and so we can know of them without seeing them. We can be aware of the greater complexities of people by being more aware of their many dimensions. We can have a larger view of Creation than just the limited one we have had so far. And we can see how we ourselves are far more complex and multi-faceted than we might have believed so far, which shows us that death of this earthly body is really no great thing in the overall, multi-dimensional existences we have as part of the Numinous. These make interesting points to ponder.

By the way, Unity, Limitlessness, and Energy remind us that everything is energy, so that dark matter is really energy just like dark energy is, and the Numinous is the Source of all of it, maybe by being the Source of the vibrations of the superstrings that form the basis of all that is. So the Numinous is both visible matter with its related invisible energy, as well as dark matter with its related dark energy, and this means that there is even more to understanding the Numinous than the complexities of the lighted forms. The Numinous is so far beyond us that pure science cannot answer all the questions, and we need Intuition to keep us aligned spiritually. After all, as great as it is to know how a star functions, it is far more important to recognize that the Numinous is at the center of it, for our spiritual lives are the most important aspects of our existence here, which we will see in the final chapter, both of our lives and of this book.

CHAPTER ELEVEN

● ● ● ● ● ● ● ● ● ●

Earthly Applications of the Factor

The Three Original Questions

Now let us return to our earthly lives and the three big questions that began this book: "Who are we? Why are we here? Where are we going?" Basically the composite answer to all three is that we are multi-dimensional, multi-universal facets of the Continuity of the Numinous who have always existed and will continue to exist as aspects of the Eternal Spirituality. Our true identities are not so much as individual human beings or even as individual spiritual beings, but as part of the Oneness of the Numinous where we achieve our fullness. We still do not know why we are here, but one basic purpose could be to participate in the growth of the creative aspects of the Numinous as we achieve Enlightenment by functioning at increasingly higher levels of consciousness, and to help others in accomplishing the same thing.

So our purpose in this book is not to understand scientific theories that will constantly change and adapt, but to see the great Truth of the Oneness of the Universe, adopt the Unity of Everything in the Numinous as part of our experience here, and dedicate ourselves to assist those around us in the growth philosophy. Through this spiritual view, we will arrive at seeing the Universe as a living, pulsating thing, expanding and contracting just as plants germinate, grow, flower, and die, their physical constituents then used to create more physical plants or even animals that feed on the plants. We will see the overview of stars continually being born, growing, then waxing old and passing on, their materials to be used in other stars elsewhere. We will see that all is in motion, all is growing, all is energy, and nothing is lost. When we see Spirituality as the moving force of all of this, much as how the black matter in space that we cannot see has a role in moving and interacting with the matter that we can see, we will have Enlightenment.

Human Applications

This means that, if we look at a human being, we can see the outer physical form, but we know that there is much more beneath the surface. We sense a multi-dimensional, extremely complex entity that is bewildering even in the physical part that we can observe. For example, the human body is made up of cells and they all have complex ways of multiplying, of burning food for energy, of eliminating waste, of protecting themselves from attack, and the like, many of which operate independently from the brain that we generally regard as the seat of intelligence in the person. We cannot see all this going on just as we cannot see the latent power of a rock, but we know that cells work in those ways because we have been able to study their actions. However, we still do not know what the breath of life is that animates them and gets them to function. We do not know from where the intelligence comes that lets them function as they do. And we do not even know why all of this is so. Therefore, we certainly do not know what the breath of life is that makes the whole Universe function, no matter how much we may learn about how it all seems to work physically.

We do remember that the most important thing about dealing with a person is seeing him as a whole, complete spiritual being because this is seeing the Numinous in him. Seeing him as needy and requiring our assistance to correct some supposedly erroneous condition denies his fullness as a facet of the spiritual and puts too much strength in our pitifully limited powers to understand and judge others. Considering him as an enemy or a person who deserves no respect denies the spiritual nature he has even though we may not approve of his actions or thoughts. It is our level of spirituality that is on the line, not his.

It is obvious that people, as well as animals and plants, have variations in their make-up, as part of their existence as different facets of the Numinous. Sometimes we criticize these variations in body or thinking as not being right according to our biased judgment. We see others as wrong in their political or social thinking; in their choices in such areas as clothes, work, associations, spending habits, and even religion; and in their physical conditioning and health habits. We tend to see them as imperfect as compared to what we perceive as perfect. Such viewpoints as these can cause a lot of unsettled feelings and even ill-will toward others, all of which is wasteful. People are as they are in their own manifestations of the Numinous, and it is up to us to recognize that through Unity.

Healing

In addition to that, it is easy to see people (and animals and plants) around us as being afflicted with illnesses, deformities, and inadequacies. We see people as being in poverty, with poor relationship skills, misguided, or on lesser levels of our ideas of perfection. Now, it can be generally accepted that the first of these, illness, can be a painful and discouraging detriment to a happy existence since it can debilitate the body, depress the mind, and misdirect growth, and cause an early demise. Good health seems to be important because the proper flow of energy in the body is akin to the flow of life. Orientals know that blockages of the flow of life's energy can lead to sickness and inability to function properly. The other elements in the lists above, however, are earthly or social judgments and may or may not have spiritual implications, so we will not consider them here. The spiritual view is to see all people as whole, complete, and perfect as exactly who they are right now because we do not know most of what makes them up in the first place, and are only seeing them from our earthly, biased, limited viewpoints in the second place. But illness deserves a special look.

The Principle of Energy reminds us that energy is the basis of everything. Therefore, ways to maintain good health through proper energy flow throughout the body are important. Preventative means are the most vital because they help keep the body and mind in top condition. But when disease does set in, two kinds of remedies may be in order. One could consist of medical treatments, medicines, lab analyses, consultations with specialists, and use of state-of-the-art treatments and equipment. The other can consist of holistic medicine, consultation with spiritual practitioners, medicinal herbs, self-help meditations, and the like. Both have their values. Requesting spiritual help from another person can certainly be in order so long as the patient remembers that each person is still responsible for his or her own health. The person who continually turns to another to heal the problems in his life through any of various means will continue being dependent on that person to heal him over and over if he does not take steps to correct the deficiencies in his body and mindset. Both medical people and spiritual practitioners should reach beyond the stated problem and help the individual to take charge of his or her own personal health and habits.

We remember that the physician sees the inner physical workings of a person and tries to deal with them in curing that person of a disease, but even the physician does not know exactly how this healing comes about because he does not really do it. He only sets the stage for it to happen through Intention. Continuity reminds that nothing has a cause, but rather that all things operate as part of the infinite manifestations of the Numinous. True healing comes through the spiritual nature, which is the person's reality. So, in dealing with people's needs on a spiritual level, restoring the person's ability to function independently in spiritual growth should be the aim. The spiritual nature of the person is made up of the full energy of the Numinous, with the physical body just one aspect of the totality. The mechanical processes of healing are a means of restoring the full flow of living energy to the body. The spiritual processes, such as the ones in this book, are the means of restoring a full flow of living energy to the spirit. When we realize just who we are and the temporary role that our limited body has in this earthly sphere, we will set our sights on a much higher healing that will be more valuable in the long run.

One way to do this is to help the person see and control personal emotional reactions, since these have big effects on the body and the choices made in life. Since the infinite facets of the Numinous encompass all levels of feeling and understanding, we do have choices that we are allowed to make. Being happy, being unhappy, being angry, being bored, being jealous, or being helpful, are all personal decisions. No one else can make us angry, for example. Anger is a luxury that we allow ourselves. If a car pulls in ahead of us on the freeway so that we have to hit our brakes to avoid a collision, we can either react with road rage or just ignore the situation and give up a little space for safety. It is our decision. Barring chemical imbalances, we are responsible for our feelings. If we say that some other person has made us angry, we are giving up control over ourselves and are allowing the other person to manipulate us, which turns us into puppets rather than spiritual beings in charge of our own growth toward Enlightenment. The act of depending on other people or on material things for our happiness is allowing the waves of possibility to collapse according to what others want, and robs us of our personal growth. Hanging on to what others think of us for our self-esteem makes us try to be what every other person wants us to be, which steals our ability to achieve oneness with the Numinous as being our own facet of infinite manifestation and, instead, makes us a copy of someone else's growth.

Choices have Karma, or consequences, of course, and we grow as we face them. As an example, the person who is constantly angry tends to have the immune system stifled, which can lead to various diseases, a field called psychoneuroimmunology. The person who decides to stay happy and balanced finds joy in everything around and imparts this to others, tending to have better health. This is the person who is approaching Enlightenment by raising personal vibrations and reaching out to help raise the vibrations of others, whereas the person who is constantly angry or critical or centered continually on personal problems is dealing in lower vibrations and therefore rejects other people or feels cut off from them, and can easily have poorer health since the personal immune system is suppressed by constant angers or anxieties. A spiritual consultant (which is what we all can be) can do well to devote some healing time to raising the sights and feelings of the petitioner to higher levels, regardless of the specific problems that caused the consultation.

The Key Is in Helping Others

Here is another key point. Both the medical practitioner and the spiritual practitioner not only give valuable assistance to society by helping others, but they also help themselves rise in spirituality when they reach out to serve. We can look at a true story to give us a little insight into this viewpoint. A high school religion teacher went back to college to start work on a Master's degree and took a philosophy course. In the first class, the professor asked each student to name their religion and describe it in one word. Students gave such descriptive words as love, joy, and salvation, and each term was met with a scathing attack by the professor that destroyed and ridiculed the concept to the great discomfort of the students. His aim, of course, was to free them from old patterns so that he could show them new ways of thinking. When it was the turn of the high school teacher, he described his religion as service. The professor reflected a few seconds, then nodded in agreement and went on to the next student. It is hard to argue against service. Selfishness leads people and animals to devour each other, whereas service leads them to support and uplift each other. Nature is rife with instances of animals helping each other. So learning to give service may be another reason why all of us are going through this earthly experience. Let us look at two ways of supporting others spiritually.

But let us establish a mindset before we look at those two ways. Spiritual consultants need to keep personal opinions out of the picture when helping others. Assuming that everyone on earth should have perfect health or that a specific problem in a specific person should be treated right now can actually impede the other person's overall growth in life's journey. It is far better to help raise spiritual consciousness in general to the point where we all are achieving what we ourselves really need. This takes a great openness to higher vibrations and intuition.

This is also why truly spiritual work has no money attached. A person who is receiving pay for spiritual work may find it difficult to concentrate fully on higher consciousness with the materialistic right there in front of them. The spiritual and the materialistic just do not mix well. The world of money, which represents earthly power, accumulation, and accomplishment, is on a different plane than is the spiritual. It might be difficult for a healer to concentrate fully on the healing process if the spirituality of the moment is mixed with thoughts of income. It might be difficult for a spiritual speaker not to "count the house" during the talk or activity, calculating the potential take from the size of the audience. This split in concentration can detract from the intensity of the message, and might even lead a speaker or healer to say only what people want to hear in order to increase the intake. It also might lead the person being treated to measure mentally just how much spirituality they have the money to afford. True spirituality has no price because the truly spiritual person already has everything that could be wanted.

There is another aspect of healing to keep in mind. We have to see that our earthly knowledge is very narrow and limited in scope compared to the vastness of the Creations of the Numinous. In our limited perspectives in this material world, we tend to forget Unity. It is always interesting, in spiritual work, to hear people speak of a disease as an error that needs to be fixed, as though the microbes that bring it and the body in which the disease occurs were not both a part of the Numinous in the first place. After all, bacteria dominated the earth for millions of years before other forms of life came along, and certainly the Numinous is familiar with what happens when bacteria invade a body. To call this an error is to deny overall spiritual truth by putting our human judgments first. Illness and decay are part of life. If fungi did not break down the trees that fall in the forest, soon there would be no room for other trees to grow and no fertile soil for them to use. No sooner does science eradicate one disease than a bunch of new ones crop up. Continuity includes every shade of purpose and experience. If we try to shortcut this, having a personal view that everybody has a right to complete and constant health, prosperity, and happiness, we may be pushing an inappropriate cookie-cutter mentality onto everyone or letting our personal opinions allow us to miss a part of the overall Plan. After all, there are many people in different parts of the world who have very little access to health or prosperity. They certainly have as much value as anyone else and are part of the Plan, so we cannot think that ill health or poverty are negatives, but rather as obstacles that are part of the infinite number of paths through life toward a common goal.

We also might easily forget that happiness is a personal decision or state of mind. We cannot make another person happy and, by the same token, we cannot make them get well. We should not feel that we have to take over and make decisions for them to solve their problems. Even if our help is requested for a specific situation, we have to keep the overall advancement of the person in mind and the responsibility they themselves bear for their own growth. In addition, physicians know that the drug treatment for a specific problem might well bring on unwanted side-effects and cause other problems, so he uses his judgment carefully. Likewise, the person doing spiritual work for healing may be part of the overall plan of healing for the sick person, but needs to be careful in evaluating the whole situation and not help bring on unwanted side effects such as allowing a dependency on his efforts or setting intention on things that are actually not beneficial in the long run.

So how should the healer working in the spiritual field carry out the work? There are two ways to do this. The best method to use is one in which the actual problem has no bearing on the treatment and, indeed, should not even be mentioned to the health practitioner. The one doing the healing service would spend most of the time allotted in seeing the other as a whole, complete, balanced person with all aspects of life in the harmony and perfection that are right for this point in time, with no thought given at all to any apparent physical or financial condition. This vision should be kept until there is a sense that all is as it should be. Since everything is always as it should be in the Numinous, this means removing our own blockages to proper spiritual vision. After all, since everything is Numinous, if anything needed to be different, it would be. Healing and improvement done at this level are, indeed, of the highest aspects of LOVE, the Level of Veritable Enlightenment. The other way is that, through our being kind, forgiving, sound, balanced, and benevolent with the other person and picturing all humanity as being the same, we actually raise the collective subconscious just a little bit including that of the person we are serving, and that is of value to all of Creation. Let us consider that briefly.

Collective Unity

The idea of raising the collective subconscious has a big role. There seems to be a relationship between rising vibrations with positive values, and falling vibrations with destructive aspects. This has been commented on and measured by subjective means for a long time. Since we know that everything is vibrating energy, and since we know from the Higgs Field that higher energy or mass are imparted to bodies or particles accelerating (not just passing) through it, and since we know that absolute zero is the temperature at which all molecular activity is supposed to stop, we draw the corollary that higher vibrations are more productive than lower ones along a sliding scale of values. Introducing high vibrations seems to raise low vibrations. If we put a bridge between a beaker of ice and a beaker of boiling water in a chemistry lab, will the cold travel to the heat, or will the heat travel to the cold? The answer is that the heat will travel to and warm up the cold since cold is just the absence of heat. It is the warmth of the higher vibrations of the sun rather than the cold of outer space that allows life and growth as we know them. Heat is at a higher vibration than cold, and so the human interpretation is that warm, nurturing vibrations will help overcome cold, destructive ones. Therefore, whatever higher vibrations people can add to the collective consciousness of the human race will help raise the level for everyone. As an example, a smile or word of praise can brighten the life of a sad or weary person and raise their personal vibrations just a little so that they may pass on the favor to another, and so it goes. Anger, criticism or ridicule can be destructive to the fragile feelings of others and are of low vibrations. Teaching, inspiring, or just listening with warmth and compassion can raise the spirits of both the giver and the receiver. Trying to allow health and happiness to come to someone who lacks them is in the same category. These acts go beyond rationality in their elevating effects on everybody, another illustration of how the true benefits of the Numinous cannot necessarily be accessed through logic alone.

This leads us back to the tantalizing concept of dimensions that we looked at earlier. Seeing a person in four-dimensional spacetime may give us a physical idea about them, but ignores the other dimensions of their being, such as their emotions, their mental processes, or their spirituality. We do not see these even though the person may be right there before us. People have other dimensions that give meaning, character, and value to them, but we only glimpse these from time to time and can never get to know the wholeness of the other person, just as we cannot know everything about a particle, according to the Heisenberg Uncertainty Principle. We could easily believe that these dimensions do not exist, just as many people do not believe that other dimensions exist outside of our familiar four or that anything exists outside of our Universe. But the person who sees the Numinous in everything can see the concept of these dimensions and has greater knowledge and ability to relate to the person and to the Universe. The mechanistic aspect, then, lacks meaning, and is only a set of observations. The real value is in the personal and, ultimately, the spiritual, and that is the purpose of the Numinous Factor. The more we learn about the healing of the body, the better, and the more we learn about the functioning of the Universe, the better, but we need to recognize the spiritual role in all of this for there to be any real meaning or value.

We must remember that we humans are located on a planet that was created out of space stuff and is now rotating around a modest star in a modest galaxy lost in a sea of billions of galaxies, all of which are expanding away from each other after a violent explosion forced them apart, all subject to the four fundamental forces as well as the influence of the Electromagnetic Field and the drag of the Higgs Field, among others. We are part of something much bigger than we are, and certainly are not the center of attention of the whole Universe. After all, the first life that developed on this earth was bacteria, which ruled the earth for millions of years, as we have seen, and then there evolved gradually other life forms such as humans who are now wondering about what is out there and where they came from, the questions that started this whole book. The answers to those questions would be fairly blah from just a mechanical viewpoint, but when we look at our ability to be aware of the spiritual aspect, the answers are more exciting.

Nothing gets true value by being a separate entity but by being one Entity in and through the Numinous. The constant Continuity that we see as the basis for all is an ongoing thing, whereas people look for things such as human life to start and stop, and then they worry about how to prevent the latter. We do not have to get caught up in all of that. It is all part of the plan because Unity and Energy remind us that all is energy and all is spiritual and none of that can be destroyed. Environmentalists who are fighting to stop material development in some areas because of endangered species may not realize that most of the species that have ever lived on this earth are now gone, and that change and new growth are part of Continuity. (But the cockroach is still here!) Everything keeps going, even though the outward aspects might change. Therefore we humans will keep going, and how we are now will certainly change, especially since we do not yet know all of our dimensions. The spiritual is bigger than the human race, the secular is really part of the spiritual, and the Numinous embodies both.

So motion and change are constants, and we just adapt to that concept, letting ourselves change form when our earthly bodies die, knowing that, as part of Energy and the Numinous, we actually go on forever in one form or another and in dimensions that we do not even fathom yet. In fact, we are probably living out many different existences in different universes at this very moment, since none of our choices in life nor those of others are ever lost, and so we all live out each of the resultant existences. Death, the cessation of an animating spirit in our body, the ceasing of all motion, thus means nothing, and we have zero to fear from it.

Motion is the norm, and higher vibrations will bring up lower ones. So the raising of vibrations to a point where a person goes beyond rationalizations, earthly desires, and destructive personal traits into a state of pure spirituality should be the goal for those who are ready to recognize Enlightenment, and again shows how true spiritual work for others never carries a price tag that would relegate it to just a material level. Participating in the physical world is valuable, but having awareness of the spiritual world is priceless.

Some Basic Questions

Let us consider some basic questions that might arise from seeing the Numinous, the Spiritual nature of everything.

Should we worship the Numinous? It certainly seems that Man has an inherent desire to worship something. Perhaps it is because mankind realizes the basic weakness of humankind and the uncertainties in life here on the planet, and tries to find a higher power to align with for safety and stability. This leads to all sorts of worship practices and the accompanying angst about whether one has done enough to ward off an eternal life of suffering. A little reflection on the Numinous will show the answer to the question. Worship implies duality, with the person here adoring a separate Being there. Since the Numinous is in, as, and through everything that exists, there is no duality. There is no requirement for worship because the Numinous does not need it, being complete in everything. And since the person is the Numinous, it would be like worshipping oneself. Rather, the person should rise in awareness to take as full an advantage as is possible at this point of identification with the Oneness in everything and find the peaceful bliss that such an acquaintance brings.

Does the Numinous answer petitions and deal in the affairs of people? We should remember that any thoughts and requests that we may have are already a part of the Numinous through the Omniconstant. A petition or a request would indicate a duality, with a petitioner appealing to a grantor, and since the Numinous is already the Essence of everything that exists, no petitions are necessary. However, we certainly have the freedom to express ourselves in life and to do what we can in helping others. What is needed, then, is for us to set our intentions, and also help others set their intentions, on achieving the highest level of consciousness possible so that the very best outcomes, which already exist in wave forms, have the propensity to manifest in this universe at this time. It might be well to use EMILY to open ourselves a little more to the spirituality already within us, allowing it to grow in Unity and Limitlessness for the good of all, and then sense the proper resolution through Intuition.

To give us a little more idea of what these advanced perspectives are that we can rise to, let us look at the energy of the Universe. The gas Hydrogen is the basis for the fusion reactions that account for much of the immense heat in the stars. The hydrogen atom is made up of one proton and one electron, and the helium atom has two of each. When the process gets going, two hydrogen atoms fuse into one helium atom, but there is a lot of energy left over, which radiates as intense heat. So there is immense energy in something as simple as one proton and one electron, and when multiplied by the vast amounts of atoms in a star, the amount is staggering. We have Unity with that power when we pause in our daily lives to reflect on it. Humans cannot deal with or create even a tiny amount of that energy, and if we think that we do, we have to realize that we are not creating anything at all, but rather are just harnessing or transforming something that already exists. Energy still applies: an electron is just energy, a proton is just energy, its quarks are energy, the fundamental strings that make up the quarks are just vibrating energy, and Intuition shows that it is the Numinous that supplies the energy to keep these things operating and makes up the protons and electrons out of this energy in the first place. No matter how much we think that we know, we cannot create anything. We can only temporarily transform or organize that which is already there, and we do not even grasp much of that anyway because our personal senses, such as eyesight, are limited. But through the Numinous, we are one with that energy and will always exist with it, even though we do not understand it very well right now.

But the spiritual world is something else. We can understand much of it through constant application of the Five Principles of EMILY: Enlightenment, Meditation, Intention, LOVE, and Yielding. And by using

Limitlessness, Unity, Continuity, Intuition, and Energy, we can understand enough of the Five Principles of LUCIE to open our awareness to the Infinite Oneness of The Numinous and grasp the peace and fulfillment of Its Totality. We can react to our feelings and practice the acts that raise our vibrations and the vibrations of others as a practical way to realize the Numinous. And we can expand beyond earthly limited knowledge from the human viewpoint to glimpse such things as: increased dimensions in ourselves and in others; our fulfillment in other universes; and the ability to recognize our personal Oneness with All that Is to find amazing peace and joy in our opportunities to grow and raise our consciousness levels as we rise through our personal Higgs Fields to spiritual levels that we cannot imagine even yet. Then we will see the value of the Numinous Factor in leading us to the Numinous Oneness.

About the Author

Dr. Walker's seventy-plus years of experience include being a professor of both religion and languages, university administrator, religious leader, prison religious counselor, public speaker, author, and mystic. He and his wife, Corky, both musicians and radio hams, enjoy Southern California life.